Week commencing **MONDAY, NOVEMBER 9th, 1936**

NIGHTLY at 7-30.   MATINEE: THURSDAY at 2-30

ANMER HALL presents

"BUSMAN'S HONEYMOON"

A NEW DETECTIVE COMEDY
By DOROTHY L. SAYERS and M. ST. CLARE BYRNE

Cast:

Mr. Puffett	ROGER MAXWELL
Bunter	NORMAN V. NORMAN
Mrs. Ruddle	NELLIE BOWMAN
Harriet	VERONICA TURLEIGH
Lord Peter Wimsey	DENNIS ARUNDELL
Miss Twitterton	CHRISTINE SILVER
Frank Crutchley	BARRIE LIVESEY
Rev. Simon Goodacre	MARTIN LEWIS

[Programme continued overleaf

Page of programme of first performance of 'Busman's Honeymoon' on 9 November, 1936 at the Birmingham Theatre Royal, signed by both authors.

DOROTHY L. SAYERS: NINE LITERARY STUDIES

TREVOR H. HALL

1980
ARCHON BOOKS

First published in 1980 in England by
Gerald Duckworth & Co. Ltd. London
and in the U.S.A. as an Archon Book
an imprint of
The Shoe String Press Inc.
995 Sherman Avenue
Hamden, Connecticut 06514

ISBN 0–208–01877–8

British Library Cataloguing in Publication Data

Hall, Trevor Henry
    Dorothy L. Sayers, nine literary studies.
    1. Sayers, Dorothy Leigh—Criticism
    and interpretation
    823′.9′12   PR6037.A95Z/

    ISBN 0–208–01877–8
    LC 80–65485

*Printed in Great Britain
by Unwin Brothers Limited
The Gresham Press Old Woking Surrey*

CONTENTS

ILLUSTRATIONS

For Marguerite

INTRODUCTION

This small collection of essays makes no pretence to be a life
of Dorothy L. Sayers. Two biographies, Janet Hitchman's
Such a Strange Lady (London, 1975) and Alzina Stone Dale's
Maker and Craftsman: The Story of Dorothy L. Sayers (Grand
Rapids, Michigan, 1978) are already in print, whilst a third is
promised by James Brabazon. For similar reasons, I have not
attempted to compile a check-list of her published work, although I am frank to say that some of the pages that follow are
not devoid of bibliographical and textual criticism. *An Annotated
Guide to the Works of Dorothy L. Sayers* (New York, 1977) has
been published by Robert B. Harmon and Margaret E. Burger,
and a more technical work of this kind is promised by Mrs
Colleen Gilbert. My purpose can be defined by the expression of
a modest hope that the odds and ends of information assembled
may be of some small assistance and interest to future students of
Miss Sayers' work, which has come very much to the forefront of
literary interest in recent years. At opposite ends of the scale, her
stories have been dramatised for television audiences and
adapted as radio plays, and dissertations on her work have been
submitted in support of applications for Ph.D. degrees.

One of the things I have tried to do is to record in print for the
first time some recollections and impressions of Dorothy L.
Sayers that have come my way from friends who enjoyed the
privilege of her acquaintance in years gone by. I have devoted
the invaluable memories of Colonel John H. Taylor, C.B.E.,
D.L., T.D., who knew both Miss Sayers and her husband in
Kirkcudbright, to the essays 'The Nebuly Coat' and 'The
Documents in the Case', to which they properly belong. As an
example of the value of 'the remembrance of things past' on the
part of another friend of mine, Charles F. Tebbutt, M.A., F.S.A.,
we may notice that on page 27 of *Such a Strange Lady* Mrs
Hitchman tells us that Miss Sayers disliked all games, although

we cannot help but notice that she is shown watching a cricket match in the photograph opposite page 129, or fail to recall the excellent account of the Pym's/Brotherhood's game in *Murder Must Advertise.*

Charles Tebbutt, a well-known archaeologist and the author of the parish history of the Huntingdonshire village of Bluntisham, spent much of his boyhood at his home there, The Walnut Trees. Miss Sayers' father, we recall, was the parish priest at Bluntisham from 1897 to 1917, and it was during the later years of his incumbency that his only daughter was an undergraduate at Somerville College, Oxford. The Walnut Trees was the only house in the village with a tennis court, where Dorothy L. Sayers used to play. In two letters written to me, in confirmation of our conversation in May 1978 at Charles Tebbutt's home in Wych Cross, Sussex, he wrote:

> My recollections of her are of her coming to our house to play tennis on Saturday afternoons, when our tennis court, the only one in the village, was more or less open to anyone in the village in a general invitation, to turn up to play. I think it unlikely that she would have had a personal invitation but would know that she would be welcome, so she must have come voluntarily. It would almost certainly be between 1910 and 1914, and I am fairly certain that I played in sets in which she took part. I am afraid I do not recollect how good D.L.S. was at tennis, or how keen. However, some measure of this lies in the fact that she came, on her own, on an open general invitation to tennis players in the village, to which there was no compulsion to accept or refuse.

Of his general memories as a boy of Miss Sayers all those years ago (the memories of a historian) Charles wrote to me:

> My recollection is that she did not make a very good impression in the village, which was strongly non-conformist. I well remember that I was told that she was a student at Oxford—women university students were rare in rural communities then—and I recollect vividly the word 'Blue-stocking' being used. This I thought an odd name, and as a boy could make no sense of it at the time. I think my parents considered that she was aggressively 'modern', and did not approve. My brother remembers our father coming home from a village fête (it may have been a church fête in the rectory garden) full

of indignation with D.L.S., who was taking some part in it. My father *would* be indignant in those days at a *woman* less than half his age daring to dispute something he had said!

I first became acquainted with the detective novels of Dorothy L. Sayers in those uneasy years preceding the outbreak of the Second World War, and was immediately captivated. My standards were high, because I had been a Sherlock Holmes enthusiast since I was a schoolboy. Even in those distant days, however, it seemed to me clear that a new writer had emerged, herself a keen admirer of the work of Sir Arthur Conan Doyle, who had created in the person of Lord Peter Wimsey an amateur investigator who was bound to become an outstanding figure in the long history of detective fiction. I think it highly significant that in recent years, thanks to the devoted work of Lt. Col. Ralph L. Clarke and his circle of fellow-enthusiasts in Witham, the Dorothy L. Sayers Historical and Literary Society has proudly taken its place beside the Sherlock Holmes Society of London.

During all the post-war years of my professional life I enjoyed re-reading the Dorothy L. Sayers books on my shelves, with that peculiar pleasure one obtains from the opening of a well-loved book after a sufficient interval. One knows in advance that it is splendid, but the details have become sufficiently hazy to make the turning of every page a delight. It is an experience that can be likened to meeting an old friend to talk over old times and shared adventures.

In 1975, thanks to the fortunate accident of being invited to deliver a lecture in Churchill College, I met Wilfrid Scott-Giles, who lives in Cambridge. He had known Miss Sayers from 1936 for the remainder of her life. In company with the late Mrs Scott-Giles and Helen Simpson, he was able to help her with the first of the two delightful privately printed pamphlets of 1936 and 1937, designed as Christmas presents for her friends. Both *Papers Relating to the Family of Wimsey* and *An Account of Lord Mortimer Wimsey, the Hermit of the Wash* are now rare and valuable, and can fairly be described as the hope and the despair of the Sayers collector. Through the generosity of an old friend, the late Frank Beckwith, the former Librarian of the Leeds Library, copies of both had fallen into my hands. Wilfrid and I found much in common, and became firm friends. We both joined the Dorothy L. Sayers Society, and visited Witham together on a number of occasions.

Wilfrid's charming book, *The Wimsey Family*, published by Gollancz and based partly on his correspondence with Miss Sayers and partly on his skill and experience in heraldry and genealogy as Fitzalan Pursuivant Extraordinary of the College of Arms, has become a success both here and in America. It had its roots in his address to the Dorothy L. Sayers Historical and Literary Society at the Seminar in Witham in 1976. The first essay in the present work is loosely adapted from my own talk to the Society at the Seminar in 1977, which was itself stimulated by an address delivered by Dr Barbara Reynolds in Witham in the previous year.

The seventh essay in the book, 'Dorothy L. Sayers and Robert Eustace', is by far the longest. It was first stimulated by Mrs Hitchman's remark on page 75 of *Such a Strange Lady* that the death of 'Robert Eustace' had never been traced, and that his inexplicable disappearance was an appropriate accompaniment to his equally mysterious life. These speculations are intriguing, but in my opinion the facts are of even greater interest. As I have remarked in the opening paragraph of 'Dorothy L. Sayers and Robert Eustace', Mrs Hitchman's comment 'will introduce to the reader (as it did to me over three years ago) one of the most fascinating literary puzzles it has been my good fortune to encounter'. The truth in regard to 'Robert Eustace' is so extraordinary that its publication is in my view essential, not only to students of the work of Dorothy L. Sayers but also to bibliographers and librarians. The importance of the inquiry is underlined by the fact that it discloses many errors in the *British Museum General Catalogue of Printed Books* and its American counterpart, the *National Union Catalog*, based on the Library of Congress. It is fortunate that Halkett and Laing's *Dictionary of Anonymous and Pseudonymous Literature* is under revision at the present time in preparation for a new edition, and that the Editor has accepted the evidence and conclusions I have placed at his disposal. Of equal importance, perhaps, so far as Sayers students are concerned, is that the solution I have offered to the mystery of 'Robert Eustace' may explain the otherwise extraordinary conduct of Miss Sayers in regard to her acknowledgement of the technical help she received in the writing of *Have His Carcase*.

It remains my pleasant duty to thank those friends whose advice and help has made this little book a pleasure to write. They include Peter A. Bond, who has been my right hand in the necessary inquiries in London, Leonard Beck, the Keeper of Special Collections in the Library of Congress, James Brabazon, with whom I have profitably exchanged information, Dennis Cox, the Brotherton Librarian of the University of Leeds and John C. T. Oates, the Deputy Librarian and Reader in Historical Bibliography in the University of Cambridge. Sir Hugh Greene and Dr Eliot Slater have been my stimulating correspondents on the subject of 'Robert Eustace'.

My special thanks are due to Lt. Col. Ralph L. Clarke, who supplied me with all the information I needed from the archives of the Dorothy L. Sayers Historical and Literary Society, and with his charming wife Molly has made the visits to Witham of my wife and myself so enjoyable. I am grateful to Percy H. Muir, my co-author in another field of interest, and to Peter Grose, who sent me details of an invaluable document. The recollections of past years, kindly sent to me by Muriel St Clare Byrne, have been indispensable, as have those of Col. John H. Taylor and Charles F. Tebbutt. My thanks are due to the Curator and Librarian of the' Marion E. Wade Collection at Wheaton College, Illinois for help gladly given to me. My special gratitude is due to Wilfrid Scott-Giles for his wise counsel and his suggestion that I should write this book, and for the enrichment of my Sayers collection by the generous gift of material which would otherwise have been unobtainable.

Selby, N. Yorks.

T.H.H.

I

LORD PETER WIMSEY AND SHERLOCK HOLMES

O N 27 November 1976, I was privileged to attend a Seminar of the Dorothy L. Sayers Historical and Literary Society at Witham, Essex, and to listen to Dr Barbara Reynolds' admirable paper 'The Origin of Lord Peter Wimsey'. Dr Reynolds made and developed two interdependent points of great interest. First, Wimsey was a *literary* inspiration, and that in order to discover his origins and to understand Dorothy L. Sayers as a writer it is a waste of time 'to ferret among the details of her personal life. To appreciate fully what she wrote, it is necessary to read what she read.' Secondly, the speaker said that Miss Sayers' Wimsey novels owed a very great deal to E. C. Bentley's *Trent's Last Case*, first published in 1913. Dr Reynolds quoted an extract from an undated manuscript draft of a short talk intended for broadcasting by Dorothy L. Sayers, preserved in the Marion E. Wade Collection at Wheaton College, Illinois, entitled 'Trent's Last Case'. In it Miss Sayers said, 'Every detective story writer of today owes something, consciously or unconsciously, to its liberating and inspiring influence.'

I am wholly in accord with Dr Reynolds' opinion that the inspiration of the Wimsey stories was literary. I am not at variance with her belief in the significance of Miss Sayers' remark, which I deliberately paraphrase (fairly, I hope) by saying that every detective story writer after 1913 owes something to Philip Trent. This is a curiously precise echo of a comment by T. S. Eliot in his five-page essay, 'Sherlock Holmes and his Times', published in *The Criterion* of April, 1929, 'that

1

every writer owes something to Sherlock Holmes', adding: 'Every critic of the novel who has a theory about the reality of characters in fiction would do well to consider Holmes.'

Eliot certainly followed his own advice, as I tried to show in the chapter 'Thomas Stearns Eliot and Sherlock Holmes' in my book *Sherlock Holmes and His Creator*. In his *Murder in the Cathedral*, first published in 1935, the first six lines of the dialogue between Thomas à Becket and the Second Tempter were copied *verbatim* (apart from three words) from the questions and answers of *The Musgrave Ritual*, the document that gave its name to one of Holmes' earliest cases, first published in *The Strand Magazine* of May 1893. In 1939 Eliot's *Old Possum's Book of Practical Cats* was published. It was a witty collection of light verse, and included a poem of 42 lines, 'Macavity: The Mystery Cat'. I was able to demonstrate in *Sherlock Holmes and His Creator* that Eliot's description of Macavity was simply that of Dr James Moriarty, the master criminal of the Holmes adventures of *The Final Problem* and *The Valley of Fear*. I summed up the resemblances, indeed, by remarking that according to Eliot it would appear that if we were able to see Macavity and Moriarty together we would hardly be able to distinguish one from the other apart from the fact, perhaps, that Moriarty was clean-shaven and that Macavity, like most cats, was not.[1] In 'Gus: The Theatre Cat', the poem following 'Macavity', Eliot used an incident from *The Empty House*, the first Sherlock Holmes story of the *Memoirs*, involving Colonel Sebastian Moran, the 'second most dangerous man in London'.

Touches of Holmes appear in many of Eliot's poems. In 'East Coker', first published in *The New English Weekly* in 1940 and later in *Four Quartets*, published in 1944, he used as a common noun the word 'grimpen', a word that is not listed in the row of massive, all-embracing volumes of *The Oxford English Dictionary*. Yet Eliot used it. He used it in his metaphor to mean some physical hazard that could exist, in this case within the precincts of a dark wood, into which the traveller might sink or fall, since, as Eliot put it, there 'is no secure foothold'. We remember

[1] This exactitude of resemblance was accepted by Lord Snow in his review of my book in the *Financial Times* of 12 May 1979.

that the Grimpen was the name given by Doyle to the great and deadly mire on Dartmoor that was, with Baskerville Hall, the topographical centrepiece of *The Hound of the Baskervilles*. Any doubt as to whether Eliot had read Doyle's masterpiece is demolished by the 'Baskerville Hound' which 'will follow you faster and faster, and tear you limb from limb', in the poem 'Lines to Ralph Hodgson, Esquire', which originally appeared in *The Criterion* of January 1933 and later in 1936 in Eliot's *Collected Poems*, 1909–1935.

The purpose of the preceding paragraphs has been to endorse Dr Reynolds' first point that great writers are frequently inspired by the work of those who have gone before them, by showing that T. S. Eliot owed much to Conan Doyle. The principal aim of the present essay, however, is to extend Dr Reynolds' second point regarding Miss Sayers' obligation to *Trent's Last Case* by demonstrating that like T. S. Eliot, she was also much influenced by the work of Sir Arthur Conan Doyle in the creation of her Wimsey stories.

In my opinion she was mischievously honest enough, at the outset in her work in this field, to plant two deliberate clues pointing unmistakably to her indebtedness to Sherlock Holmes. I point first to Holmes' address of 221B Baker Street and Wimsey's flat at 110A Piccadilly. If we divide 221 by two, the result is 110 and one over. A is the first letter of the alphabet. For the second deliberate clue, we must look at the first edition of the first novel written by Dorothy L. Sayers, *Whose Body?*, published in 1923 by T. Fisher Unwin in London and by Boni and Liveright in New York. In both these first editions a secondary title, 'The Singular Adventure of the Man with the Golden Pince-Nez', appears on A4 recto before the first page of the text. It follows the half-title, the title-page and the dedication of the book to 'M. J.', addressed to 'Dear Jim'. In parenthesis, it is a pleasure to record my indebtedness to Miss Muriel St Clare Byrne, who kindly identified 'M. J.' for me as the late Muriel Jaeger, who was at Somerville with Dorothy L. Sayers.

The secondary title of 'The Singular Adventure of the Man with the Golden Pince-Nez' was not repeated in any of the subsequent editions (as opposed to impressions) of *Whose Body?* It is possibly a flight of fancy (and possibly not) to imagine

Miss Sayers, later to be founder and a President of the Detection Club, saying under her breath:

> This is my first detective novel, and in this and those that I hope will follow I shall play fair with my readers. I will give the second clue to my indebtedness to Sherlock Holmes once only to readers of *Whose Body?*, on both sides of the Atlantic, and that should be sufficient.

It is at least one explanation of the curious incident (to use a Sherlockian phrase) of the non-appearance of the secondary title after the *editio princeps*. Its existence is now unknown to many because of the extreme scarcity of the first edition of *Whose Body?*

The significance of the clue of 'The Singular Adventure of the Man with the Golden Pince-Nez' lies in the fact that it is pure Baker Street, and that 'singular' must surely be regarded as one of the favourite adjectives used by the creator of the most famous consulting detective in literary history. On the second page of the first of the short stories, *A Scandal in Bohemia*, Watson tells us of Holmes' 'clearing up of the singular tragedy of the Atkinson brothers at Trincomalee', and on the facing page we are told how Holmes stood before the fire and looked Watson over 'in his singular introspective fashion. "Wedlock suits you," he remarked'. On the third page of *The Copper Beeches*, during a discussion between the two friends in regard to Watson's method of recording the cases, reference is made to his unspoken thought that egotism was an ingredient in Holmes' 'singular character'. On the very next page the earlier affair of *A Case of Identity* is recalled by Holmes as 'the singular experience of Miss Mary Sutherland'. We recall that among the early cases investigated by Holmes before Watson became his Boswell, and listed for us in *The Musgrave Ritual*, was 'the singular affair of the aluminium crutch'.

In *The Five Orange Pips*, Watson's list of the cases solved during the year 1887 included 'the singular adventure of the Grice Patersons in the island of Uffa'. It was in *The Red-Headed League* that an example was recorded of how, in Holmes' 'singular character', his extreme exactness and astuteness represented the reaction against the poetic and contemplative mood that occasionally predominated in him. The examples I have quoted are sufficient to document the point, and to enable us to extend our inquiry by an examination of the text of *Whose Body?*

In the first chapter of this first book about Wimsey, Lord Peter describes his introduction to his first case as 'Enter Sherlock Holmes'. There are references to the sage of Baker Street in Chapters 7, 9, and 11. The second of these further examples is of special interest, since it sums up the traditional relationship in this kind of literature between the gifted amateur and the professional police force, originated by Edgar Allan Poe, and developed by Doyle. We have to remember that in *Whose Body?* Inspector Parker's later relationship by marriage to Wimsey, and their close friendship, was not foreshadowed. Wimsey had already obtained broad confirmation of his own theory regarding the identity of the murderer by consulting Sir Julian Freke's entry in *Who's Who*. The receipt of a telegram at Denver from Inspector Parker, expressing complete puzzlement over the case, naturally delighted Wimsey, who exclaimed that it gave him confidence in himself. 'Makes me feel like Sherlock Holmes. "Perfectly simple, Watson".' He added for good measure that he felt ready to take on Professor Moriarty if necessary.

It is of interest to notice the result of Wimsey's examination of a letter in Chapter 5:

> Good parchment paper, printed address of a solicitor's office in Salisbury, and postmark to correspond. Very precisely written with a fine nib by an elderly business man of old-fashioned habits.

This can be compared with a typical Baker Street quotation from *The Greek Interpreter*, used as a test question in Ivar Gunn's examination paper on Sherlock Holmes, and quoted by both Desmond MacCarthy and Vincent Starrett:

> Here it is, written with a J pen on royal cream paper by a middle-aged man with a weak constitution.

In Miss Sayers' second novel, *Clouds of Witness*, published by T. Fisher Unwin in 1926, her devotion to the literature of Baker Street is just as obvious. The name of Sherlock Holmes appears in

Chapters 6, 9, 11 and 15. In Chapter 11 Wimsey is actually described as 'the Sherlock Holmes of the West End'. Dr Watson is mentioned by name in Chapter 13. The account of the almost fatal adventure in the treacherous bog, Peter's Pot, in Chapter 12, must surely remind us of the deadly Grimpen Mire in *The Hound of the Baskervilles*. In the same chapter Wimsey, on discovering the all-important letter from his brother wedged in the bedroom window-frame at Grider's Hole, described himself to his manservant Bunter as being, without exception, the biggest ass in Christendom. This can scarcely fail to recall to our memory a similar observation by Holmes to Watson in the affair of *The Man with the Twisted Lip*:

> I think, Watson, that you are now standing in the presence of one of the most absolute fools in Europe.

Having considered the evidence of the first two Wimsey novels, it is of interest to jump forward nearly twenty years to see if Dorothy L. Sayers was still influenced by Sherlock Holmes in her last detective story *Talboys*, written in 1942 but not published until 1972. In this final problem Miss Quirk draws attention to the damp mould on the boots of Bredon Wimsey, the elder son of Peter and Harriet, as evidence in the mystery of the missing peaches. Wimsey prefixes a short discourse on what is and what is not garden mould, and the necessity of some practical training even for the work of a purely domestic detective, by the remark to Miss Quirk: 'Elementary, my dear Watson.' Miss Sayers thus placed in the mouth of her aristocratic detective, in the very last story she wrote about him, one of the best known quotations in the world. The interesting fact that the precise phrase, 'Elementary, my dear Watson', actually appears nowhere in any of the 56 short stories and 4 long stories about Sherlock Holmes does not affect the point that the influence of the literature of Baker Street was with her to the last as it had been from the beginning. We recall, moreover, that Wimsey used the phrase more than once. He used it, for example, on the infuriated and love-sick Willis in the fourth chapter of *Murder Must Advertise*, first published by Victor Gollancz in 1933, about half-way between the dates of *Whose Body?* and *Talboys*.

There are too many striking similarities between Holmes and Wimsey to be coincidental. Holmes, like Wimsey, was of gentle birth. We know from the text of *The Greek Interpreter* of his descent from a long line of English country squires, and that his grandmother was the sister of H. Vernet (1789–1863), the third of a line of great French painters. Even as a Cambridge undergraduate, Holmes felt entirely at home at Donnithorpe, the Trevors' great country house in Norfolk. He was equally at ease in Colonel Hayter's gun-room in *The Reigate Squires*, with Reginald Musgrave at the manor house at Hurlstone in the case of *The Musgrave Ritual*, and with Lady Brackenstall at *The Abbey Grange*. Holmes displayed no embarrassment in dealing with such clients as Lord Cantlemere in regard to *The Mazarin Stone*, or with Lord Holdhurst or the Duke of Holdernesse, K.G., P.C., in the affairs of *The Naval Treaty* and *The Priory School*. He treated with respectful but easy courtesy Wilhelm Gottsreich Sigismond von Ormstein, Grand Duke of Cassel-Falstein and hereditary King of Bohemia.

In *The Hound of the Baskervilles* Watson observed of Holmes, who had been living in a prehistoric stone hut on Dartmoor:

> He had contrived, with that cat-like love of personal cleanliness which was one of his characteristics, that his chin would be as smooth and his linen as perfect as if he were in Baker Street.

This fastidiousness is surely echoed throughout the Wimsey books by the bathroom scenes and the attentions of Bunter. We recall that in *Busman's Honeymoon* Peter invites Harriet to feel his chin, her verdict being, 'M'm—yes—like satin.'

Wimsey was always exceedingly well-dressed. We remember that in the fourth chapter of *Whose Body?* Lord Peter and the Hon. Freddy Arbuthnot looked like an advertisement for gentlemen's trouserings as they strolled into the dining-room of Wyndhams. It is difficult to forget the description of Wimsey as a marvel of sleek elegance in 'The Entertaining Episode of the Article in Question' in *Lord Peter Views the Body*, and the tone-symphony in monochrome formed by his spats, light trousers and exquisitely polished shoes. Even if Watson had not reminded us in *The Musgrave Ritual* that his famous fellow lodger always 'affected a certain quiet primness of dress', we would have remembered those wonderful illustrations by Sidney Paget, which so perfectly harmonised with the narratives, and always showed the great detective perfectly attired for the occasion. We recall the illustration opposite page 76 of the first edition of *The Hound of the Baskervilles* showing Holmes and Watson, pictures of sartorial perfection in top-hats and frock-coats, walking down Regent Street. The fact that the plate is printed the wrong way round, showing Paget's signature in mirror writing and the London traffic on the wrong side of the street, does not detract from the splendid overall impression. In field investigations away from Baker Street, Holmes favoured his immaculate travelling cloak, spats and deer-stalker, as depicted in the two well-known railway carriage scenes in *The Boscombe Valley Mystery* and *Silver Blaze* on pages 79 and 2 of the first editions of the *Adventures* and the *Memoirs*.

Wimsey was interested in and knowledgeable about food and wine. 'The Bibulous Business of a Matter of Taste' in *Lord Peter Views the Body* recalls his identification of the vintage of seventeen wines whilst blindfolded, against a bet with Freddy Arbuthnot at the Egotists Club. In the same episode the Comte de Rueil compliments Wimsey by saying that there could not be six men in the world with a palate such as his. In *Unnatural Death* we read on the first page of the extraction of a bubbling-hot Helix Pomatia from its shell. Later in the same book, when the scene has changed from an exclusive Soho restaurant to Epping Forest and a case of death by poisoning, Wimsey identifies a sandwich wrapped in greasy newspaper as containing treacle-cured Bradenham ham. In *The Unpleasantness at the Bellona Club* Wimsey composes a dinner for Ann Dorland consisting of Huîtres Musgrave (oysters fried in their shells with little strips of bacon), *tortue vraie* soup, filet de sole ('the merest mouthful'), *faisan rôti* with *pommes Byron* and a salad, with a bottle of 1908 Romanée Conti and a *soufflé glacé* to finish the meal.

Sherlock Holmes was also a gourmet. We remember the splendid dinners at Marcini's and Simpson's described in *The Hound of the Baskervilles*, *The Illustrious Client* and *The Dying Detective*, and the 'little supper' at Baker Street which included 'a couple of brace of cold woodcock, a pheasant, a *pâté-de-foie-*

gras pie, with a group of ancient and cobwebby bottles', consumed at the end of the case of *The Noble Bachelor*. The impromptu midday snack enjoyed by the two friends during the action of the affair of *The Veiled Lodger* consisted of a cold partridge and a bottle of Montrachet. During the case of *The Sign of Four*, Holmes insisted that Inspector Athelney Jones should join Watson and himself at Baker Street for a meal of 'oysters and a brace of grouse, with something a little choice in white wines'. When the cloth was cleared, Holmes helped his friends to an admirable port. "One bumper," said he, "to the success of our expedition. And now it is time we were off".'

The first thing we learn about Wimsey in the first chapter of *Whose Body?* is that he was a book-collector. When the case opened, he was about to attend a book auction to bid for the first Florence edition of Dante, a 1481 folio by Nicolo Lorenzo. It is stated in a footnote on page 13 that Wimsey's collection of printed Dantes contained several examples of the greatest rarity. His entry in *Who's Who* tells us that he was the author of *Notes on the Collection of Incunabula*, and that his recreations were criminology, bibliography, music and cricket.

There can be no possible doubt that Sherlock Holmes, like Wimsey, was an enthusiastic and knowledgeable book-collector. During the very first case recorded by Watson, *A Study in Scarlet*, Holmes shows his friend what he describes as 'a queer old book I picked up at a stall yesterday—*De Jure inter Gentes*—published in Latin at Liège in the Lowlands in 1642'. I cannot resist adding my own personal admiration, because research shows that this item was almost certainly unique. Wing and other bibliographers of the period give the date of the first edition of this rare work by Richard Zouche as having been published in Oxford in 1650. Holmes' Liège edition is not listed in de Montjardin's *Bibliographie Liègoise* (Bruxelles, 1867), nor in the second or *Deuxième édition augmentée* of the same work of reference, published in Bruges in 1885. In *The Sign of Four*, when Watson admonished Holmes in regard to his drug habit, the great detective 'raised his eyes languidly from the old black-letter volume he had opened'. In *A Scandal in Bohemia* Watson said that after his marriage to Mary Morstan he saw little of Holmes, who 'remained in our lodgings in Baker

Street, buried among his old books'. We know that Holmes' concern with book-collecting was life-long, for during *His Last Bow* Watson remarked: 'But you had retired, Holmes. We heard of you living the life of a hermit among your bees and your books in a small farm upon the South Downs'.

His entry in *Who's Who* apart, we have positive evidence that Wimsey was a musician. Like the book collection, the grand piano was a feature of the Piccadilly flat. We need perhaps remember no more than the word picture in the final chapter of *Gaudy Night*, through the eyes and mind of Harriet Vane, of Wimsey listening to the Bach Concerto in D Minor for two violins at the Balliol concert, and the scene in *Strong Poison* in which Wimsey plays the Italian Concerto for Miss Murchison. We recall their subsequent taxi journey together to White-chapel Road during which Wimsey would talk about nothing but music, and in particular fugal form, rather than the real object of the expedition, which was to teach Miss Murchison how to pick a lock. In parenthesis, I would remark here upon Holmes' similar ability completely to detach his thoughts temporarily from the criminal cases in which he was involved. During the train journey to Ross-on-Wye in *The Boscombe Valley Mystery* he remarked to Watson:

> No, sir, I shall approach this case from the point of view that what this young man says is true, and we shall see whither that hypothesis will lead us. And now here is my pocket Petrarch, and not another word shall I say of this case until we are on the scene of action.

Even when the scene of action had been reached, and the two friends were installed in the Hereford Arms with the preliminary inquiries completed, Holmes said:

> Those are the crucial points upon which the case depends. And now let us talk about George Meredith, if you please, and we shall leave minor points until tomorrow.

Holmes, like Wimsey, was a musician. His Stradivarius violin was a feature of 221B Baker Street, and it was to music that he normally turned when restful detachment from intellectual effort became necessary. We remember *The Red Circle:*

Well, Watson, you have one more specimen of the tragic and grotesque to add to your collection. By the way, it is not yet eight o'clock, and a Wagner night at Covent Garden! If we hurry, we might be in time for the second act'.

We recall Watson's description of the afternoon at St. James's Hall during the action of *The Red-Headed League*, following Holmes' suggestion that his patients could spare him for a few hours. Watson wrote:

'My friend was an enthusiastic musician, being himself not only a very capable performer, but a composer of no ordinary merit. All the afternoon he sat in the stalls wrapped in the most perfect happiness, gently waving his long thin fingers in time to the music.

Two other examples of invitations to Watson of this kind are sufficient. They occur respectively in *The Retired Colourman* and *A Study in Scarlet*:

Let us escape from this weary workaday world by the side door of music. Carina sings tonight at the Albert Hall, and we have still time to dress, dine and enjoy.

And now for lunch, and then for Norman Neruda. Her attack and her bowing are splendid. What's that little thing of Chopin's she plays so magnificantly? Tra-la-la-lira-lira-lay.

I should perhaps mention that Watson's omission of the hyphen in Norman-Neruda can be confusing to the casual reader. She was of course Lady Hallé. 'Tra-la-la-lira-lira-lay' has been provisionally identified by experts as the Nocturne No. 15 in F minor.

A final point of very great interest in regard to Wimsey, Holmes and their shared deep interest in music occurs in the conversation between Peter and Harriet at the Balliol concert, after the last movement of the concerto in D Minor has ended. Wimsey says that he likes his music polyphonic. It is surely a surprising coincidence that Watson should tell us in *The Bruce-Partington Plans* that in 1896 Holmes was responsible for the writing of a 'monograph upon the Polyphonic Motets of [de] Lassus, which has been printed for private circulation, and is said by experts to be the last word on the subject'.

A final astonishing point of similarity was first drawn to my attention by my friend C. Wilfrid Scott-Giles. Between 1891, the year of *The Final Problem*, and 1894, the year of *The Empty House*, even Watson was convinced that Holmes had died in company with Moriarty at the Reichenbach Falls, after a fatal struggle between the great detective and the master criminal. Holmes spent this period in Italy, Tibet, Persia and France, allowing nobody but his brother Mycroft to know that he was alive, and instructing Mycroft to preserve the Baker Street rooms exactly as they had always been, awaiting Holmes' return. The object of this elaborate three-year deception was the ultimate rounding up of the remnants of Moriarty's criminal organisation, and in particular Colonel Sebastian Moran, described by Holmes during Moriarty's lifetime as 'the second most dangerous man in London'. As Holmes told Watson during the action of *The Empty House* after the arrest of Moran (and after Watson had recovered from his only fainting fit in his life precipitated by Holmes' miraculous return from the dead) the trial of the Moriarty gang three years previously had left Colonel Moran at liberty, a situation that must be remedied at all costs. Moran, who had been the best shot in India, still possessed the wonderful air-gun, noiseless and of tremendous power and accuracy, made specially to the order of Moriarty by Von Herder, the blind German mechanical genius.

It will be remembered from the text of 'The Adventurous Exploit of the Cave of Ali Baba', in Miss Sayers's *Lord Peter Views the Body*, that Wimsey indulged in a similar subterfuge with complete success. His death while shooting big game in Tanganyika was officially reported and his will proved at £500,000. Wimsey remained ostensibly dead for two years, the object of the deception being the arrest of the fifty members of the criminal organisation referred to as 'the Society', and ruled with a Moriarty-like iron hand by an anonymous master-mind known simply as 'No. 1'.

Wimsey accomplished this by joining 'the Society' himself (he became 'No. 21') posing to his sponsor as Joseph Rogers, a footman dismissed for stealing from his last position, but possessed of valuable knowledge of large houses occupied by persons of great wealth, ripe for burglary. Like Holmes, he made careful plans for his ultimate return to his normal life at

110A Piccadilly as Lord Peter Wimsey by taking Bunter into his confidence, and in his ostensible will leaving him the lease of the flat and an annuity of £500 per annum. The remainder of the will completed these necessary arrangements. After some bequests to charity, he bequeathed to his mother, the Dowager Duchess, the remainder of his estate, including the valuable collection of books and pictures he had accumulated. Wimsey's mother and sister were aware that he was still alive, but they knew nothing of 'the Society', or his activities connected with it. However, Bunter was fully informed, and had a vital part to play when the critical moment arrived.

Wimsey had prepared a book containing the details he had obtained of every member of 'the Society' during his connexion with it, which he kept in a strongroom of ingenious mechanism in the house in Lambeth where he lived as the supposed ex-footman. When his disguise was penetrated Wimsey contrived to induce 'No. 1' to go to Lambeth to retrieve the book, armed with the combination 'UNRELIABILITY' for opening the strongroom, in exchange for the guarantee of the lives of Wimsey's mother and sister and a quick death for himself. There was, however, rather more to the strongroom than the secret of opening it. It was self-closing. 'No. 1' found himself trapped in an unventilated chamber, which could only be opened by the words 'Open Sesame' spoken by Wimsey himself. The closing of the strong-room door, moreover, gave a signal to Bunter which sent him to Scotland Yard. The police arrested every member of 'the Society', and Wimsey jubilantly remarked to Inspector Charles Parker, 'I've got the great big top Moriarty of the whole bunch quietly asphixiating at home.'

This remark demonstrates that Wimsey was well aware of the similarity of his campaign against 'the Society', and Sherlock Holmes' pursuit of Moriarty and his followers. He may well have found some additional satisfaction from the circumstances that by careful planning he had rounded up 'No. 1' and the whole of 'the Society' in one operation, whereas Holmes had found it necessary to fight two battles against crime to complete his victory over the Moriarty organisation, separated by three years. 'The Adventurous Exploit of the Cave of Ali Baba' resounds with Holmesian echoes, and I find it impossible to believe that when Miss Sayers was writing this story the shadow of the Reichenbach was not lying across her table. Indeed, when she chose this story as an example of her own work in the second collection of *Great Short Stories of Detection, Mystery and Horror* she may well have been deliberately acknowledging her indebtedness to Sherlock Holmes and his creator.[1]

I conclude this essay with an expression of gratitude to Dr Barbara Reynolds, whose splendid paper on Dorothy L. Sayers and *Trent's Last Case* inspired me to write it. My belief is that we are both right in thinking that Dorothy L. Sayers owed much to both E. C. Bentley and Sir Arthur Conan Doyle. I think the point is well demonstrated by Miss Sayers' 40–page Introduction to the first Gollancz collection of *Great Short Stories of Detection, Mystery and Horror*, which has been judged by many to be the best short history of the detective story as a literary form ever written. It may be thought significant that Miss Sayers devoted three enthusiastic pages to *Trent's Last Case*, which she described as 'an acknowledged masterpiece', and three-and-a-quarter equally laudatory pages to the work of Sir Arthur Conan Doyle under the headline 'Sherlock Holmes and His Influence'. The only two other writers of detective fiction to which Miss Sayers devoted substantial discussion were Edgar Allan Poe and Wilkie Collins.

[1] Wimsey was stated to be 37 at the date of his assumed death. He was born in 1890, according to his entry in *Who's Who* appended to the later editions of the Wimsey novels. Wilfrid Scott-Giles and I share the view that 37 is almost certainly a misprint for 34, and that the action of 'The Cave of Ali Baba' started about 1924. An assumption that Wimsey's supposed death occurred in 1927 means that any attempt to construct a chronology of his cases is doomed to failure, as experiment will demonstrate.

II

DOROTHY L. SAYERS AND
SIR ARTHUR CONAN DOYLE

WHEN the University of Durham conferred the degree of
D.Litt., *honoris causa*, upon Dorothy Leigh Sayers, the
Public Orator said of her:

> It may fairly be asserted that her detective novels have collectively
> given more pleasure to educated readers than any since Conan
> Doyle's immortal series. Both authors present the personality and
> circumstances of their characters so vividly that the accessory details
> sometimes count even more than the main story. By this subtle
> means their stories become vehicles of their own attitude to society
> and its problems, material and moral; and a penetrating criticism of
> these matters is implanted in the guise of an idle tale.
>
> This breadth of outlook and of human sympathy is well known to
> be in Miss Sayers the basis of a moral strength, in which a lively and
> uncompromising Christianity is the central core. At a given moment
> the novels were laid aside in favour of an earlier interest in religious
> truth, and this was expressed in a stream of stimulating essays and
> plays and at length in a vigorous and painstaking verse translation of
> Dante's *Inferno*.

I must say that I am at amiable variance with the Public
Orator in the assessment of stories of the calibre of *The Nine
Tailors* and *The Hound of the Baskervilles* as 'idle tales'. I agree
wholeheartedly, however, that Miss Sayers and Sir Arthur
brought to vivid life, in a fashion few if any other exponents of
the detective novel have achieved, the fascinating characters
who lived at or visited 110A Piccadilly and 221B Baker Street.

Miss Sayers was fully aware of the effectiveness of Doyle's narrative power as early as 1928. In her Introduction to the first collection of *Great Short Stories of Detection, Mystery and Horror*, which she edited for Victor Gollancz, she compared to great advantage the atmosphere of 221B Baker Street, exemplified in a quotation from *The Musgrave Ritual*, with Edgar Allan Poe's description of life in the grotesque and gloomy mansion occupied by Auguste Dupin and his anonymous chronicler in *The Murders in the Rue Morgue*. She wrote that the sturdy independence of Watson added salt and savour to the eccentricities of Holmes, compared with the flavourless hero-worshipping self-abnegation of Dupin's friend. She pointed out, too, how the concrete details of daily life in Baker Street lifted the stories out of the realm of the fantastic, and gave them solid reality.

In my opinion, there is a distinct parallel between the literary careers of Miss Sayers and Conan Doyle, a similarity that extends to their attitude towards the detective story after each had achieved such striking success in this field, and the importance of religious belief to both of them in their later work. I should perhaps say that Doyle's enthusiastic acceptance of spiritualism as a religion at the age of 57, subsequent to the period of materialism that had followed his rejection of the teachings of his strict Jesuit education, is as much a puzzle to me as it was to the late John Dickson Carr, the author of *The Life of Sir Arthur Conan Doyle*. My view of the world, like that of Carr, is not a magical one, but I recognise that religion is a subjective matter, and that there can be no doubt whatever that during the last fourteen years of his life Doyle believed in the teachings of spiritualism as fervently as Miss Sayers embraced the orthodox faith of Christianity. Doyle said in his autobiography, *Memories and Adventures*, published in 1924, that spiritualism had come to absorb the whole energy of his life. Doyle said that getting its teachings across to others was a task that would occupy, either by voice or by pen, the remainder of his years. Doyle might have been right about spiritualism, or (as I think) he may have been wrong about it, but there cannot be the slightest doubt about his complete belief in it.

In the chapter 'Conan Doyle and Spiritualism' in my *Sherlock Holmes and His Creator* I placed the date of Doyle's conversion

16

to spiritualism as October 1916, when he announced his belief in communication with the dead in the spiritualist magazine *Light*. Doyle himself said that he begun his campaign in 1916 in his autobiography (p. 396). In my book I have presented the case, based on Doyle's correspondence with the Editor of *The Strand* and other evidence, that the stories published as *The Case-Book of Sherlock Holmes* had been written at an earlier date and discarded, and that *His Last Bow*, published in *The Strand* in 1917, was correctly named. In this view I have the support of John Dickson Carr, who wrote in *The Life of Sir Arthur Conan Doyle* (pp. 315–17):

> Even without our private knowledge of the author's state of mind, we can feel in the texture of *His Last Bow* that it is more than another adventure of Sherlock Holmes. It was, as the author subtitled it, an 'epilogue'. It was to be, really and finally, *His Last Bow* ... It is the last thrill, the final drumbeat, the apotheosis of Sherlock Holmes. The whole series should have ended with *His Last Bow*, as the author formally and finally intended it to end.

It is of interest to recall that when Doyle was a young doctor in Southsea in the 1880s he met an enthusiastic spiritualist, Major-General A. W. Drayson, and attended a few séances. Under the persuasion of F. W. H. Myers, Doyle joined the S.P.R. in 1893. This temporary interest was soon overlaid, however, by that historic day in 1886 when Doyle settled down at his desk to write *A Study in Scarlet*, the first of the sixty stories about Holmes and Watson, which were to enrapture his public and make Doyle's fortune. The parallel between the remark of the Public Orator at Durham about Miss Sayers' work, 'At a given moment the novels were laid aside in favour of an earlier interest in religious truth', and Doyle's violent renewal of interest in spiritualist faith in 1916, can scarcely be denied.

Astonishing as it may seem in retrospect, both Doyle and Miss Sayers found difficulty in finding publishers for their first detective novels. Doyle tells us in his autobiography that he started to write *A Study in Scarlet* in March 1886 and completed it one month later. He sent it to James Payn, the Editor of *Cornhill*, who returned it with the verdict, 'too long for a story, too short for a book'. Frederick Warne and Arrowsmith also refused it. Finally, Ward, Lock & Co. said that they would be willing to include it in their *Beeton's Christmas Annual* at the end of the following year, 1887, but would only pay £25 for the complete copyright with no royalties. Doyle accepted these meagre terms.

Doyle's difficulty in finding a publisher for *A Study in Scarlet* is echoed, or so it seems to me, in Miss Sayers' essay, 'Gaudy Night', contained in *Titles to Fame*, edited by Denys Kilham Roberts and published in 1937. This is, in my view, one of her most important and revealing pieces of writing about her approach to the detective novel as a literary form. She said of her first novel, *Whose Body?*, that 'the book eventually (with what labour, O Prince, what pain) found a publisher'. This phrase makes it clear that there was an appreciable interval between the completion of *Whose Body?* and its publication by T. Fisher Unwin, for which *The English Catalogue of Books* gives us a date of October 1923. In *Titles to Fame* Miss Sayers tells us that she 'set out, fifteen years ago, to write the first "Lord Peter" book'. *Titles to Fame* was first published in October, 1937, according to the verso of the title-page and *The English Catalogue of Books*, and one might normally except that Miss Sayers' essay would be written in 1936 to allow for the normal processes of printing, proof-reading by ten authors, illustration and binding. On this interpretation, Miss Sayers' 'fifteen years ago' would give us 1921 as the year when she 'set out' to write *Whose Body?* This is the year firmly stated by Mrs Hitchman on pages 61–2 of *Such a Strange Lady*:

> After many stops and starts the book was finished in 1921 and offered to several publishers who turned it down on the grounds of 'coarseness' . . . . Dorothy eventually managed to sell the book to Fisher Unwin. They were taken over by Benn, who finally brought it out in 1923.

The matter is not free from complication, for there is some internal evidence to suggest that Miss Sayers' essay 'Gaudy Night' in *Titles to Fame* was written or amended in proof in 1937. In an 18-line footnote on page 88 she refers somewhat critically to 'the quaint reception given in the Press to my

'I STOOD AS ONE ALREADY DEAD.'

(*See page* 80)

Canterbury play, *The Zeal of Thy House'*. This was first performed at the Canterbury Festival and reviewed in *The Times* of 14 June 1937, and was published in book form by Victor Gollancz in the same year. Miss Sayers also quoted *verbatim* seven lines from her novel *Busman's Honeymoon* published in June 1937, although in this instance I concede that the equally quotable page-proofs were in existence in 1936, for I possess a copy in wrappers with that date on the title-page. It is probable that an absolute solution is not possible, but I am frank to say that I prefer the inferential date of 1922. Such a choice would give us the pleasing coincidence with Doyle's wait of 1886 to 1887 between the completion and publication of his first Sherlock Holmes novel. Whether 1922 or 1921 is right[1], we can say that we know within a year the beginning of Miss Sayers' pre-occupation with Lord Peter Wimsey, and her 'avowed intention' (I quote again from *Titles to Fame*) of following in the footsteps of Wilkie Collins in the construction of detective stories that were to be novels of manners as opposed to pure crossword puzzles.

I remarked in the final paragraph of the preceding chapter that Miss Sayers included a long tribute to Sir Arthur Conan Doyle in her Introduction to the first collection of *Great Short Stories of Detection, Mystery and Horror*, published by Gollancz in 1928. She wrote (p. 28):

> In 1887 *A Study in Scarlet* was flung like a bombshell into the field of detective fiction. . . . The effect was electric.

She said that Doyle had taken up the formula devised by Poe in *The Murders in the Rue Morgue*, *The Mystery of Marie Rogêt* and *The Purloined Letter*, and had galvanised it into life and activity. He had replaced the elaborate psychological introductions with crisp dialogue, and had featured prominently what Poe had only touched upon—the deduction of staggering conclusions from the observations of slight clues unnoticed by Watson and the official police. 'He was sparkling, surprising and short. It was the triumph of the epigram.'

As I had occasion to say in the first chapter of my first venture

---

[1] In the short biography of Miss Sayers on page 242 of *Titles to Fame* it is stated that she wrote *Whose Body?* in 1922.

into the Higher Criticism of the literature of Baker Street,[1] Miss Sayers' enthusiasm led her into describing *A Study in Scarlet* as a bombshell, when it must be sorrowfully conceded that it was in fact something of a damp squib. Its appearance in *Beeton's Christmas Annual*, 1887, in company with two drawing-room plays, 'Food for Powder' and 'The Four Leaved Shamrock, by R. Andre and C. J. Hamilton, did not excite any great attention. Doyle settled down to write *The Mystery of Cloomber* and *Micah Clarke*, both published in 1889, the second of which was a very considerable success. It was in this year, too, that Doyle began the intensive study of what his biographer, John Dickson Carr, described as a 'carrier's cart' of books on the Middle Ages in preparation for the writing of his great historical novel, *The White Company*, to be published two years later.

It seems possible that we might have heard little more of Sherlock Holmes had not the editor of *Lippincott's Magazine* read *A Study in Scarlet*, and thought well enough of it in 1889 to invite Doyle to write a second Holmes and Watson story. As a result, *The Sign of Four* (originally *The Sign of the Four*) was published in 1890 in both the English and American editions of *Lippincott's*, and later in the same year as a book by Spencer Blackett. It had to wait, however, for two years for a second edition.

Miss Sayers was perfectly right about the bombshell, but she was four years too early in regard to its explosion. It was the first series of short stories about Sherlock Holmes in the *Strand Magazine*, starting with *A Scandal in Bohemia* published in the issue of July 1891, that caused Holmes and Watson ultimately to become household words, comparable in the vocabulary of the man in the street with Shylock, Hamlet and Robinson Crusoe. An ingredient in this delayed success may have been, as the late Sir Sydney Roberts suggested, that 'after two false starts, the iconography of Holmes and Watson was established'[2]. With the first of the *Strand* stories came the co-operation of Sidney Paget as illustrator, whose drawings of the two immortal lodgers at 221B Baker Street, harmonized perfectly with the

[1] *Sherlock Holmes. Ten Literary Studies* (London, 1969 & New York, 1970 & 1976).
[2] On page ix of his Introduction to *Sherlock Holmes. Selected Stories by Sir Arthur Conan Doyle* (London, 1951).

spirit and atmosphere of the narratives, which blazed into popularity in 1891. A case can be made, I fancy, that Miss Sayers was momentarily thinking of *A Scandal in Bohemia* rather than of *A Study in Scarlet* when she wrote of the 'bomb-shell'. Her praise of Doyle, 'He was sparkling, surprising and short', is not applicable in its third adjective either to *A Study in Scarlet* or *The Sign of Four* which, with *The Hound of the Baskervilles* and *The Valley of Fear*, make up the collected edition of *Sherlock Holmes. The Complete Long Stories*, first published in 1929. Miss Sayers' further observation, 'It was the triumph of the epigram', suggests the same thing, since an epigram is a short and pointed saying or poem.

Direct and overwhelming evidence of Miss Sayers' deep interest in Sherlock Holmes is available to us in her book of essays, *Unpopular Opinions*, published in 1946. It contained four amusing and erudite pieces which she grouped under the general title of 'Studies in Sherlock Holmes'. In her Foreword Miss Sayers said that the game of applying the methods of the Higher Criticism to the Sherlock Holmes canon was begun, many years ago, by Monsignor Ronald Knox[1] with the aim of showing that by this procedure one could examine and treat as a corpus of research material a modern classic as speciously as a certain school of critics has endeavoured to scrutinise the Bible. It must be played, she insisted, as solemnly as a county cricket match at Lord's, since the slightest touch of extravagance or burlesque completely ruins the atmosphere. The truth of this precept is demonstrated, we may think, by comparing Miss Sayers' four urbane, tongue-in-cheek parodies of scholarly method in *Unpopular Opinions* with a regrettable piece of outlandish nonsense such as 'Watson was a Woman', contributed by Rex Stout to *Profile by Gaslight* (New York, 1944), a collection of essays by various hands edited by the late Edgar W. Smith.

In parenthesis, I think it possible that our American col-

---

[1] 'Studies in the Literature of Sherlock Holmes', first published in *The Oxford Blue Book* in 1912, and reprinted in *Essays in Satire* in 1928. Knox was in fact preceded in the exposition of the Higher Criticism of Sherlock Holmes by Frank Sidgwick's 'An Open Letter to Dr Watson' in *The Cambridge Review* of 23 January, 1902 concerning *The Hound of the Baskervilles*, and by Andrew Lang, who wrote on *The Three Students* in *Longman's Magazine*, July 1904. In an essay on Conan Doyle published in the same month in *The Quarterly Review*, Lang also amusingly applied the Higher Criticism to *The Sign of Four* and *The Noble Bachelor*.

leagues may argue that their fellow-countryman, Rex Stout, is not alone in his introduction of an element of hermaphroditism into the realms of detective fiction, and that Dorothy L. Sayers did the same thing. It is true that in Chapter XI of *Murder Must Advertise* Wimsey rather oddly addresses the notorious Miss Dian de Momerie as 'my dear Watson'. In Chapter IV of *Have His Carcase*, moreover, Wimsey not only remarks to Harriet Vane, 'These are deep waters, Watson' (which comes straight from *The Speckled Band* and *The Reigate Squires*), but on three separate occasions in the same chapter addresses Harriet as 'Sherlock', adding in the first of these examples, 'Where is the dressing-gown? How many pipes of shag have you consumed? The hypodermic is on the dressing-room table.' These are harmless lapses, however, and can readily be excused on the grounds of Miss Sayers' ever-present preoccupation with the work of Conan Doyle.

The order of the four essays in *Unpopular Opinions* is 'Holmes' College Career', 'Dr Watson's Christian Name', 'Dr Watson, Widower' and 'The Dates in *The Red-Headed League*'. The original publication dates of these pieces demonstrate the wide time-span of Miss Sayers' deep interest in the subject. 'The Dates in *The Red-Headed League*' first appeared in *The Colophon: A Quarterly for Booklovers*, Part 17, No. 10, June 1934. One month later, 'Holmes' College Career' was published in *Baker Street Studies*, a collection of essays by various distinguished hands edited by H. W. Bell, which *The English Catalogue* tells us was published in July 1934. Among other contributions was 'The Medical Career and Capacities of Dr. J. H. Watson', by Miss Sayers' friend Helen Simpson. In parenthesis, it is of great interest to remember that three years later in March 1937 Helen Simpson and Dorothy L. Sayers joined forces again. In company with Muriel St. Clare Byrne and my friend Wilfrid Scott-Giles,[1] they delivered a group of lectures on the history of the Wimsey family (another scholarly leg-pull) in Sidney Sussex, the Cambridge college which had been tentatively identified by Miss Sayers as Sherlock Holmes' *alma mater* in her essay, 'Holmes' College Career'.

'Dr Watson's Christian Name', which in my view is the most

---

[1] C. W. Wilfrid Scott-Giles, OBE, FSA, is the historian of Sidney Sussex.

brilliant of Miss Sayers' four essays exemplifying the Higher Criticism of the Sherlock Holmes Canon, first appeared in *Queen Mary's Book for India*, published in July 1943 and now a very scarce book indeed. The first two sentences of the Foreword by the Rt Hon. L. S. Amery indicate its general theme and purpose:

> This little book, prefaced by the human touch of the Queen Mother's message to the mothers of India's fighting men and happily bearing Queen Mary's name, is mainly about India. More particularly is it concerned with India's share in the world conflict and with the men and women of India who are playing so splendid a part in our common cause.

Contributors included Sir Winston Churchill, Field-Marshal Sir Archibald Wavell, Air-Marshal Sir Patrick Playfair, Commander Anthony Kimmins, the Rt. Hon. Ernest Bevin, Sir Arnold Wilson, Sir Cyril Atkinson, Sir Leonard Woolley, Walter de la Mare, T. S. Eliot (whose poem 'To the Indians who died in Africa' was not reprinted elsewhere so far as I am aware) and J. A. Spender, so that Dorothy L. Sayers and 'Dr Watson's Christian Name' were in distinguished company. It may be thought to be a literary puzzle that India is not mentioned in the essay, which is concerned to show that John H. Watson's second forename must have been Hamish, the Scottish form of James, thus accounting for Mrs Watson's addressing her husband by this name in *The Man with the Twisted Lip*.

In parenthesis, because it is a further similar example of an essay by Dorothy L. Sayers appearing in distinguished company and against an unusual background, I may mention that in my collection of her work I also have a copy of *The Etonian Review*, July 1933. The Editors, J. M. A. Gwyer and A. M. Rueff, wrote of this volume, found for me by my friend and co-author, Percy H. Muir:

> Its sole aim is to live up to its name, by providing an entertaining, if slight and fragmentary review of Eton, and, more especially, of Etonians.

The contributors included the Earl of Athlone, Randolph Churchill, the Earl of Clarendon, the Marquess of Clydesdale, Lord Dunsany, Dean Inge, Ronald Knox, Shane Leslie, Harold

Nicolson, Sir W. Rothenstein, the Master of Semphill, Earl Winterton and Dorothy L. Sayers, whose amusing essay, 'Schools for Heroes', is on pages 25–7. I think it right that these distinctions in the publication of Miss Sayers' work should be recorded in print, since neither *Queen Mary's Book for India* or *The Etonian Review* seem to be known to Robert B. Harmon and Margaret A. Burger, the compilers of *An Annotated Guide to the Works of Dorothy L. Sayers* (London & New York, 1977).

The fourth of Miss Sayers' essays on Holmes and Watson contained in *Unpopular Opinions*, 'Dr Watson, Widower', made its first appearance in print in that book, in company with her splendid definition of the Higher Criticism of the literature of Baker Street. It can be said, therefore, that her published interest in the best known work of Sir Arthur Conan Doyle persisted from 1928, when she wrote the Introducton to the first volume of *Great Short Stories of Detection, Mystery and Horror*, until 1946, the year of publication of *Unpopular Opinions*. This was four years later than her final abandonment of Wimsey, after writing *Talboys* in 1942, to be discovered and published in 1972. The MS. of 33 pages was found among her papers after her death and is now preserved in the Marion E. Wade Collection at Wheaton College, Illinois. It clearly post-dates the uncompleted sequel to *Busman's Honeymoon*, to be called *Thrones, dominations*, and announced for publication about 1939, according to James Sandoe in his 'Contribution Toward a Bibliography of Dorothy L. Sayers', published in *Bulletin of Bibliography*, May–August, 1944 and Carolyn Heilbrun in her essay 'Sayers, Lord Peter and God' in *The American Scholar*, Spring 1968. The 176 pages of the uncompleted sequel to *Busman's Honeymoon* are preserved at Wheaton College, and the clue to its abandonment may lie in the fact, we may think, that the month of publication of *Busman's Honeymoon* in England was June 1937, the month of the first performance of *The Zeal of Thy House* at Canterbury. This was, I fancy, the significant year of the parting of the ways, despite the publication of *In the Teeth of the Evidence* in 1939, which did contain two Wimsey stories, and the appearance in the same year of a collection, *Detective Medley*, edited by John Rhode, to which Miss Sayers contributed 'Striding Folly' and 'The Haunted Policeman', both featuring Wimsey. The latter story was a sequel to *Busman's Honeymoon*, since it features the birth of the first son of Peter and Harriet, as was *Talboys* with its enlargement of the family as essential to the plot.

Despite these final flourishes of Wimsey in short story form after what I regard as the fateful year of 1937, and which died out with the writing of *Talboys* in 1942, the fact remains that two of her studies in the Higher Criticism of Sherlock Holmes were first published during the four ensuing years. We recall that 'Dr Watson's Christian Name' appeared for the first time in *Queen Mary's Book for India* in 1943, and that 'Dr Watson, Widower' was first published in *Unpopular Opinions* in 1946. It is of interest that she accepted the invitation to review John Dickson Carr's *The Life of Sir Arthur Conan Doyle* in *The Sunday Times* of 6 February 1949. I must in fairness concede, however, that two years later her enthusiasm for the subject had finally given way to the religious interests that dominated her later years of literary effort. On 13 April 1951, she politely declined a flattering invitation from the Sherlock Holmes Society of London. She wrote to the Hon. Secretary:

> I feel that Holmes-worship has been a good deal over-done of late, especially in America; so that one tends to lose interest. I have added my little quota to Holmes 'research' and am pretty well played out on the subject. However, I wish you all success and many merry meetings.

An interesting similarity between the detective stories of Sir Arthur Conan Doyle and Dorothy L. Sayers is that the first editions of both are now exceedingly scarce and expensive, whilst their books on other subjects are not. It is common knowledge that one would be lucky to find a copy of *The Hound of the Baskervilles* (1902) in good condition at less than £80, but I confess to my surprise at noticing *The Nine Tailors* (1934) and *In the Teeth of the Evidence* (1939) offered in booksellers' catalogues this year at £35 and £20 respectively. More remarkable still is the price of an item quoted in Blackwell's catalogue *Rare Modern Books*, 1975. No. 180 is '(Sayers, Dorothy L.) An Account of Lord Mortimer Wimsey, the Hermit of the Wash. Related in a Letter to Sir H— G— Bart, by a Clergyman of the Church of England, "Bristol: Printed by M. Bryan, Corn-Street, 1816", (1937), First Edition, 16 pp. slim 8vo, *fine copy, folded from the sheet as issued*. Designed in the style of early nineteenth-century pamphlets and printed at the Oxford University Press. The format and appearance were designed and superintended by Mr Graham Pollard. It was printed in November and December, 1937. In all, about 50 copies were privately issued, for friends'. The price quoted for this 16-page unbound pamphlet was £140, doubtless due to its very small printing and the name Wimsey in the title, although it was not a detective story in any sense of the word.

This rare item is in my own collection. As I recorded with gratitude in the Introduction, it came to me as a gift from my friend the late Frank Beckwith, M.A., M.Phil., our former Librarian of the Leeds Library, founded in 1768, together with another pamphlet which Miss Sayers had produced for her friends, *Papers Relating to the Family of Wimsey. Edited by Matthew Wimsey*. This was a larger booklet, 55 pages in length, in blue paper wrappers, with two illustrations, and the Wimsey arms, crest and motto on the title-page. It preceded *An Account of Lord Mortimer Wimsey*, and was prepared by Miss Sayers with some assistance and printed in 1936 for presentation to friends at Christmas of that year. The help of Wilfrid Scott-Giles and other friends is mentioned in the book, and he was delighted to answer my many questions about its history. Wilfrid told me that Helen Simpson did the extracts from diaries, the trial report and the broadsheet. The late Mrs Scott-Giles was responsible for the frontispiece, the splendid portrait of the 10th Duke of Denver, and Wilfrid himself drew the Wimsey arms, the extract from Evelyn and the epitaph of the 10th Duke. The drawing of Bredon Hall is signed by W. J. Redhead, the architect who was responsible for the splendid drawing of the church of Fenchurch St. Paul and the detail of its roof which formed the frontispiece of *The Nine Tailors*. I have never seen a copy of *Papers relating to the Family of Wimsey* offered for sale.

Miss Sayers' first novel, *Whose Body?* (1923) is now a rare book both in its English and American editions. The printings would probably be small, as it was an unknown author's first novel, and many copies have probably been read to pieces or went for paper salvage during the Second World War. It is sobering thought that over forty years ago the best example of a first edition that a collector of the resources and stature of the late John Carter could find was an ex-library copy. It was listed in the catalogue, *Detective Fiction, A Collection of First and a few Early Editions*, issued in 1934 by Scribners of New York. It consisted in the main of Carter's own books, an assembly on which he had based his essay 'Detective Fiction' in *New Paths in Book-Collecting*, published in the same year and which he edited. Carter's description of No. 324 in the Scribner catalogue (he was the firm's European representative) was:

SAYERS (Dorothy L.). WHOSE BODY? London: Fisher Unwin, 1923. First English edition, blue cloth. Front endpaper missing. A clean ex-library copy. Miss Sayer's first novel and a very scarce book.

The price in 1934 was three dollars.

In parenthesis, and thanks to my friend Percy H. Muir, I can conclude the history of John Carter's copy of *Whose Body?*, which is not lacking in interest. The assembly of books in the Scribner catalogue was ultimately acquired *in toto* by the Lilly Library of Indiana University at Bloomington. This collection made an important contribution to the contents of *The First Hundred Years of Detective Fiction*, a splendidly produced and lavishly illustrated catalogue of 'An Exhibition held at the Lilly Library, Indiana University, Bloomington, July–September, 1973', with a Foreword by the late David Randall, the University Librarian. It commemorated the 130th anniversary of the first publication in book form of Edgar Allan Poe's *The Murders in the Rue Morgue* (Philadelphia, 1843). No. 68 in the catalogue, in the section 'England after 1914' is John Carter's copy of *Whose Body?*, listed by the librarian as:

Sayers, Dorothy L. *Whose Baby?* London: Fisher Unwin, 1923. Blue cloth. Detective: Lord Peter Wimsey. The author's first book. Miss Sayers was one of the first women to obtain an Oxford degree, obtaining top honors in medieval history. From this background comes the erudite nobleman detective.

The unfortunate connotation of *Whose Baby?* apart, a comment upon the 'top honors in medieval history' is unavoidable. At the rear of *Titles to Fame*, published in 1937 and already quoted in this chapter, is a short biography of each of the ten distinguished writers who contributed to the book. These must have been provided by the authors themselves (which would have been the simplest method) or checked by them. Of Miss Sayers' scholastic career it is said: 'She was educated at Godolphin School, Salisbury, and went from there to Somerville College, Oxford, where she read French and took first Class Honours in 1915.' To be certain on the point, I wrote to the College Secretary at Somerville, who kindly sent me the entry for Dorothy Leigh Sayers in the College Register:

Second Public Examination. Honours, Modern Languages, French, Class I. Trinity Term, 1915.

So far as I have been able to discover, the pretty story about Miss Sayers' 'top honors in medieval history' (with an occasional variation into 'top honors in medieval literature') was originated by Howard Haycraft in 1942, and has been copied by Tage la Cour, Harald Mogensen, Carolyn Heilbrun, David Randall, Robert B. Harmon and Margaret A. Burger during a period of over thirty-five years.

III

THE SINGULAR AFFAIR
OF THE VERSO SIGNATURE

O<small>N</small> page 79 (No. C27) of *An Annotated Guide to the Works of Dorothy L. Sayers*, Robert B. Harmon and Margaret A. Burger tell us that the essay 'Dr Watson's Christian Name' was first published in *Profile by Gaslight. An Irregular Reader About the Private Life of Sherlock Holmes. Edited by Edgar W. Smith* (New York, 1944). As we have seen in the previous chapter, this date was a year too late, as the essay had been included in *Queen Mary's Book for India*, published in 1943, a fact of which Miss Sayers' bibliographers were evidently without knowledge. They were, perhaps, misled by the editor of *Profile by Gaslight*, who in his introductory note to 'Dr Watson's Christian Name' on page 180 of his book remarked:

> In the paper which follows, Miss Dorothy Sayers makes public for the first time her own brilliant speculations on this vital issue in the significant relationship it bears to the hitherto unexplained fact that Watson was known to his wife as 'James'.

When I first read this erroneous sentence many years ago, before I found the first printing of 'Dr Watson's Christian Name', I was at least convinced of one thing. Miss Sayers had never seen a proof of it. We recall her annoyance with Ernest Benn, who published the first edition of *The Unpleasantness at the Bellona Club* with 'Dorothy Sayers' on the spine. Leigh was her mother's maiden name, and she insisted that her name was

Dorothy L. Sayers. We remember that she made the very reasonable point that other authors were not subjected to the indignity of being called H. Wells, J. Priestley or Ethel Dell.

The late Edgar Wadsworth Smith, a wildly enthusiastic American Sherlockian and a Vice-President of General Motors, sufficiently wealthy to have arranged that his postal address in Morristown, New Jersey should be '221B Baker Street', has misled some students in regard to the dating of another of Miss Sayers' essays, 'Dr Watson, Widower.' As we know from Miss Sayers' Foreword to *Unpopular Opinions*, this essay made its first appearance in that book in 1946, together with three non-Sherlockian essays in the book, 'Christian Morality', 'Forgiveness' and 'Living to Work', which had not been published before. The title of this chapter, purposefully Holmesian in its wording, refers to the clue that has led me to believe that Edgar W. Smith deliberately tried to deceive readers of one of his books that he possessed a printing of 'Dr Watson, Widower' published eleven years earlier before its appearance in *Unpopular Opinions*. This was a direct contradiction of Miss Sayers' statement that the first publication of 'Dr Watson, Widower' was in 1946, and the matter was therefore a serious one.

In 1958 *The Incunabular Sherlock Holmes* was published at Morristown, New Jersey, for The Baker Street Irregulars by Edgar W. Smith, in 350 numbered copies. It consisted of 19 essays about Sherlock Holmes by different hands, arranged in chronological order from 1902 to 1944, the sixteenth being 'Dr Watson, Widower', by Dorothy L. Sayers, with a date of *c.* 1935. In both the text and the contents page it lies between 'Prolegomena to the Life of Dr Watson', by the late Sir Sidney Roberts and a date of 1929, and 'Sherlock Holmes is Mr Pickwick', by Wilbur K. McKee, with a date of 1941. In his two and a half page Foreword, Smith asserted that the curiously irregular appearance of the text of his book, for which he claimed historical exactitude, was due to the fact that he had reproduced the original first printing of each essay in facsimile by the offset process:

> In arranging them, the pieces have been put into the chronological order of their first appearance in print so that the evolution the Canonical exegesis has pursued over the years can be roughly traced.

The disparate styles in which they are set out is the result not of any desire to achieve a deliberate diversity, but of the fact that the offset process in which this volume is done requires a facsimile reproduction of the original pages whence they were culled.

I wish profoundly that Smith were alive to defend his position, for I have no doubt whatever that 'Dr Watson, Widower' in *The Incunabular Sherlock Holmes* is simply an offset of the printed text of the essay as it was published in *Unpopular Opinions*, but given a false date eleven years too early. The precise similarity of the type and setting apart (other than the insertion of 'by Dorothy L. Sayers' below the printed title) the deception is proved by the presence on page 152 of Smith's book of three capital letters of irrefutable significance to the student of bibliography.

Unpopular Opinions is a 16mo, that is to say each of the sections of the book, formed by the gatherings of the folded printed sheets, consists of 16 leaves or 32 pages. At the foot of the first page of each gathering, below the print, a capital letter of the alphabet (called by the trade a 'signature') is unobtrusively printed in progressive order to assist the binder to assemble the gatherings in the right order. 'Dr Watson, Widower' is printed on pages 152 to 168 inclusive of *Unpopular Opinions*. As the first five gatherings of 32 pages total 160 pages, the first page of the sixth gathering is 161 and occurs in the text of 'Dr Watson, Widower'. Being an odd number it is a right-hand page as the book lies open, this applying, of course, to all modern printed books. The right-hand page is called the 'recto' and the left-hand page the 'verso'.

Since page 161 of *Unpopular Opinions* is the first page of a gathering we would expect it to have a 'signature', which it has, and we would expect in normal circumstances that it would be the capital letter 'F', the sixth letter of the alphabet, since page 161 is the first page of the sixth gathering. It has the letter 'F' printed at the left-hand end of the margin at the foot of the page, but the signature is more than that in the case of this particular book. It is 'FUO'. Printers have personal habits, like everyone else. The printers of the book, the Camelot Press Ltd, recorded the initials of the title of the book in every signature throughout the text by adding 'UO' after each letter identifying the number of the gathering. If we turn back 32 pages to the foot of page 129 we find EUO, and so on throughout the whole of *Unpopular Opinions*. I apologize for the 'toiling lucidity' of this explanation, an expression used by the late John Dickson Carr, writing as Carter Dickson, in regard to some of the expositions of mysteries by his detective, Sir Henry Merrivale. All these signatures are naturally on the recto or right-hand page of the book as it lies open. For obvious reasons, a signature can never appear on a left-hand or verso page.

In *The Incunabular Sherlock Holmes* Smith re-paginated his offset reproductions of the pages of 'Dr Watson, Widower', and his first page, bearing the title, was 143, a recto. In *Unpopular Opinions*, on the other hand, Miss Sayers had started the essay on page 152, a verso. As a result of this reversal of rectos and versos throughout the original and the offset copy, Smith's precise reproduction of Miss Sayers' page 161, bearing the signature 'FUO', becomes his page 152, a verso on the left-hand side of the book. The signature 'FUO' appears at the bottom of the offset copy, 'which is impossible' as we used to write at school in place of 'Q.E.D.' at the foot of spurious geometrical proofs in which our maths master delighted in lighter moments, and is a complete giveaway. I imagine that Smith was without any bibliographical knowledge, and had no idea that the glaring clue he had left *in situ* totally exposed what he had done.

That this fatal mistake arose from ignorance, and that Smith would have blocked out 'FUO' had he understood its overwhelming significance, is I fear unhappily demonstrated by comparing page 144 of *The Incunabular Sherlock Holmes*, the second page of the essay, with the corresponding page 153 of *Unpopular Opinions*. Miss Sayers had three footnotes at the bottom of this page, the third of which reads:

> It appears likely that Holmes was born between 1852 and 1854. On grounds given elsewhere (see my paper on 'Holmes' College Career', p. 134) I am inclined to give my preference to 1853.

Miss Sayers' reference to page 134 was of course to that page in *Unpopular Opinions*, and is in fact the first page of the essay 'Holmes' College Career'. Had Smith left the footnote intact with its reference to page 134 (which in *The Incunabular Sherlock Holmes* was the twelfth page of Smith's reproduction of Sir S. C. Roberts' 'Prolegomena to the Life of Dr Watson') the game would have been up with a vengeance. The footnote appeared in truncated form on Smith's page 144 as:

It appears likely that Holmes was born between 1852 and 1854

The damning second sentence had been blocked out before the offset copying of the page. It had not been done with care, because the full-stop that should have followed '1854' had been accidentally obliterated with the rest.

I have often wondered, and have been asked, why Smith went to all this trouble to produce a spuriously dated essay by Miss Sayers. The idea of financial gain is laughable. Smith was a wealthy man, who gave generous financial support to the Baker Street Irregulars, and went to the trouble of making available at modest prices out of print books about Sherlock Holmes that would have been otherwise unavailable to students. The idea of an elaborate leg-pull is attractive, but is not supported by the serious (even ponderous) tone of the Foreword, and the obvious usefulness to the student of a chronological list of this kind.

Book-collectors are a curious lot (I am one myself) and I have wondered if Smith could not bring himself to believe that 'Dr Watson, Widower' was really published for the first time in 1946, on the basis that 'Holmes' College Career' had been published as early as July 1934, one month after 'The Dates in *The Red-Headed League*'. He may have thought that the story *must* have appeared somewhere before, probably in a magazine, if only he could find it. He was unsuccessful, but if he had some theory about it this might account for the curious date in the 'Contents' of '*c.* 1935'. He may have thought that the forgery was merely anticipating a future discovery which he believed to be certain. It has been said that Charles Dawson, the forger of the Piltdown skull, was actuated by a similar motive, passionately believing that a genuine skull existed and would undoubtedly be found one day, so that his action merely anticipated history. He had nothing to gain financially, being a successful solicitor with an appointment as Steward of the Manor. He had already been elected an F.S.A., the highest distinction available to an amateur archaeologist and historian, and his reputation was secure.

I knew Smith only by correspondence, and found him obliging and straightforward in our few business transactions, which were limited to my purchases of the books he produced. As I have said earlier in this essay, I wish he was still alive to solve the mystery for us.

IV

THE NEBULY COAT

O<small>N</small> page 84 of his *The Collector's Book of Detective Fiction*, Eric Quayle illustrates the only three published works of fiction of John Meade Falkner (1858–1932), the distinguished author and antiquary, who became honorary librarian to the dean and chapter of Durham and hononary reader in palaeography at the University of Durham. He was a poet and a historian, his *History of Oxfordshire* being published in 1890. Unusually in the case of an antiquary and man of letters, Falkner was also extremely successful in the world of business. He became tutor to the sons of Sir Andrew Noble (1831–1915), the physicist and artillerist, who was awarded the K.C.B. for his work on gunnery and explosives to which is due the exact science of ballistics, revolution in the composition of gunpowder and the design of guns. From being tutor to Sir Andrew's sons, John Meade Falkner became secretary of his employer's company, Sir W. G. Armstrong, Whitworth & Co., and on the death of Sir Andrew finally became Chairman of the firm's Board of Directors.

Falkner's three fictional works were *The Lost Stradivarius* (1895), *Moonfleet* (1898) and *The Nebuly Coat* (1903). Mr Quayle is of the opinion that only the last of these titles can properly be classed as a detective story, although some critics have suggested that *The Lost Stradivarius* also qualifies. It is, however, only with *The Nebuly Coat* that we are concerned in the present essay.

35

In the chapter, *The Documents in the Case*, in the present work, I describe the recollections of Colonel John H. Taylor of holidays spent in Kirkcudbright with his uncle and aunt, Mr and Mrs Charles Oppenheimer, when he became acquainted with Dorothy L. Sayers and her husband. Mr and Mrs Oppenheimer owned a quite extensive library containing some detective and mystery stories, in which Miss Sayers was naturally most interested. In this collection was John Meade Falkner's *The Nebuly Coat*, which Miss Sayers took down from the shelf, with the comment that it was a book of which she was very fond and much admired. A few years later, in 1934, she was to publish *The Nine Tailors*, which many critics believe to be her best book. Since her father had been the incumbent of two Fenland parishes, Bluntisham and Christchurch, where much of her childhood had been spent and where she almost certainly wrote her first two novels, it cannot be doubted that the inspiration for the wonderful story of the mysterious death at Fenchurch St Paul, with its background of the great church, the fen country, change-ringing and the menace of floods came mainly from her own memories. On the other hand, as Dr Barbara Reynolds and I have pointed out, great writers are inevitably inspired to some extent by those who have gone before them and those whose work they have admired.

The action of *The Nebuly Coat* takes place in a small community called Cullerne, two miles from the coast, and separated from the sea by salt-marshes. The marshes are protected from the sea by a stone dyke with a sluice to let the River Cull out to sea. A combination of a spring-tide and a strong south-east wind, however, could cause the sea to come over the sea-wall. If these events coincided with heavy rainfall, the result was deep flooding, particularly of the land around Cullerne Church, which is the centre-piece of the story. Like the church of Fenchurch St Paul, the church at Cullerne was enormous, and is referred to on page 5 of *The Nebuly Coat* as 'Cullerne Minster'.

At the end of the book are four pages of musical scores, 'Tunes played by the Chimes of St Sepulchre's Church at Cullerne', and Colonel Taylor told me that when Miss Sayers took *The Nebuly Coat* from the shelf, she turned to these pages and was able to hum the tunes from the scores, spontaneously and accurately. These 'tunes', were not concerned with change-ringing, but there are plenty of references to that peculiarly English custom and colourful descriptions of it in *The Nebuly Coat*. Indeed, the bells of Cullerne Church are described on page 299 as 'the sweetest peal in all the West Country'. As I cannot imagine that those sufficiently interested to read a book about Dorothy L. Sayers will not be completely familiar with the text of *The Nine Tailors*, I do not think it necessary to quote from that masterpiece in support of the suggestion that she may have been inspired by the following passage on pages 299–300 of *The Nebuly Coat*:

How they swung and rung and sung together, the little bells and the great bells, from Beata Maria, the sweet, silver-voiced treble, to Tailor John, the deep-voiced tenor, that the Guild of Merchant Tailors had given three hundred years ago. . . . It seemed as if the very bells were glad to break their long repose; they sang together like the morning stars, they shouted of how they had rung when Abbot Harpingdon was given his red hat, and rung again when Henry defended the faith by suppressing the Abbey, and again when Mary defended the Faith by restoring the Mass, and again when Queen Bess was given a pair of embroidered gloves as she passed through the Market Place on her way to Fording. They remembered the long counterchange of life and death that had passed under the red roofs at their feet, they remembered innumerable births and marriages and funerals of old times; they sang together like the morning stars, they shouted together like the sons of God for joy.

Later on page 300 the description continues:

The ropes and the cage, and the pins and the wheels, had all been carefully overhauled; and when the day came, the ringers stood to their work like me, and rang a full peal of grandsire triples in two hours and fifty-nine minutes. There was a little cask of Bulteel's brightest tenpenny that some magician's arm had conjured up through the wheel-hole in the belfry floor; and clerk Jannaway, for all he was a teetotaller, eyed the foaming pots wistfully as he passed them round after the work was done.

'Well,' he said, 'there weren't no interrupted peal this time, were there? These old bells never had a finer set of ringers under them, and I lay you never had a finer set of bells above your heads. I've heard the bells swung many a time in Carisbury tower, and heard 'em when the Queen was set upon her throne, but lor! they aren't so deep nor so sweet as this old ring'.

Another likeness to the background of *The Nine Tailors* was that the mystery in *The Nebuly Coat* was concerned with past events in the history of the family dominating Cullerne, the wealthy, land-owner Lord Blandamer living at Fording, the great house of the neighbourhood. The coat-of-arms of the Blandamers, the 'nebuly coat', was depicted on the great window at the end of the church transept, and the centre 'seemed to suggest a shield of silver-white crossed by waving sea-green bars'. The organist of Cullerne Church, Nicolas Sharnall, tells queer stories about the shield and its capacity for good or evil influence, and of a local man, Martin Joliffe, unstable and poverty stricken, who to the date of his death claimed that he had proof that he was the real Lord Blandamer and the true owner of Fording. The credibility of these stories is not diminished by the fact that Lord Blandamer marries Anastasia, the sister of the ill-fated Martin.

The 'detective' in *The Nebuly Coat* is an architect named Westray, who is engaged upon a survey of the church because of fears for the safety of the tower, in which cracks have appeared in the tower arches. It is Westray, who has been regaled with the stories about the Blandamer family by Sharnall, who finds the organist's body in the organ loft where he has died in mysterious circumstances. The loft is lit by moonlight streaming through 'the great window at the end of the south transept', the window of the nebuly coat.

> The moonlight that shone on the dead face seemed to fall on it through that brighter spot in the head of the middle light; it was as if the Nebuly coat had blighted the life out of the man who lay still upon the floor.

Westray's later experience in the church is of great interest, against the background of *The Nine Tailors*:

> Then he crept deafened with the clangour down the stairs into the belfry, and sat on the sill of a window, watching the ringers rise and fall at their work. He felt the tower sway restlessly under the swinging metal. Then he went down into the church, and up again

into the organ loft, whence he could see the wide bow of that late
Norman arch which spanned the south transept. . . . He thought of
that scene which had happened in this very loft, of Sharnall's end, of
the strange accident that had terminated a sad life on that wild night.
What a strange accident it was, what a strange thing that Sharnall
should have been haunted by that wandering fancy of a man following him with a hammer, and then be found in this very loft, with the
desperate wound on him that the pedal-note had dealt. . . . He could
hear the deep-voiced Tailor John go striding through the intricacies
of the Treble Bob Triples, and yet there was another voice in
Westray's ears that made itself heard even above the booming of
the tenor bell. It was the cry of the tower arches, the small still
voice that had haunted him ever since he had been at Cullerne. 'The
arch never sleeps', they said—'the arch never sleeps', and again,
'They have bound on us too heavy a burden to be borne but we are
shifting it. The arch never sleeps'. The ringers were approaching
the end; they had been at their work for nearly three hours, the
5040 changes were almost finished. But before the hum and chatter
had died out of the air, and while the red-faced ringers in the belfry
were quaffing their tankards, the architect made his way to the
scaffolding, and stood face to face with the zig-zag crack.

The end of *The Nebuly Coat* is an account of disaster, like *The
Nine Tailors*. Cullerne is assailed by a violent gale, and Westray
is anxious about the safety of the great tower of the church.
'Would the thin bows of the tower arches live through such a
night, with the weight of the great tower rocking over them?'.
The following evening, as the gale continues with undiminished
violence, ' there was a jangle of sound, a deep groan from Tailor
John and a shrill cry from Beata Maria, a roar as of a cannon, a
shock as of an earthquake, and a cloud of white dust hid from the
spectators the ruin of the fallen tower'. Lord Blandamer, who
had inexplicably entered the church, is killed in the ruins. The
previous evening Westray had confronted him with documentary proof of Blandamer's father's illegitimacy and the comple-
mentary proof of the dead Joliffe's claim to the title and estates.

V

ATHERTON FLEMING: A LITERARY PUZZLE

I N the archives of the Dorothy L. Sayers Historical and Literary Society at Witham in Essex is an account of her father's
life written in 1976 by Mrs Ann Schreurs, the surviving
daughter of Captain Atherton Fleming by his first wife. Fleming
and Miss Sayers were married at Holborn Registry Office on 13
April, 1926. Fleming, who gave his age as 43 (he was actually
44) described himself as a journalist, and 'the divorced husband
of Winifred Ellen Fleming, formerly Meyrick'. He gave his
address as 163 Hammersmith Road, Hammersmith. Dorothy L.
Sayers, who declared herself to be a spinster of 32 and of no
occupation,[1] gave her address as 24, Great James Street,
Holborn.

In her statement made to the Society, which occupies five
foolscap sheets, Mrs Schreurs defends her father's memory
against some of Mrs Hitchman's criticisms of him in her book
Such a Strange Lady. The paragraph which has the greatest
interest for me, however, from which I quote the first five
sentences, is headed:

POSSIBLE COLLABORATION

My mother believed Mac [i.e. Fleming][2] to have collaborated
considerably in the Wimsey series. When she first read one she was

[1] This was an odd description, for she had been working as a copywriter for
Bensons, the advertising agents, since 1921 and was still doing so. Her first novel,
Whose Body? had been published in 1923, and *Clouds of Witness* was published in 1926.
[2] Fleming was generally called 'Mac' by his intimates. His mother's maiden
name was Maconochie.

surprised to find the manner and mannerisms were Mac's, and most of all the flippant humour. Many people who knew father had the same impression. Someone who had read a Wimsey, knowing nothing of the writer, sent it to us, thinking Mac had written it under a *nom-de-plume*. We believed there must have been collaboration, most of the framework being Dorothy's and much of the dialogue Mac's.

The possibly too simple answer that comes to mind in conflict with this suggestion is that Miss Sayers' first novel, published in 1923 (and probably written about 1922, four years before her marriage to Fleming), had already established the characters of Wimsey, his mother the Dowager Duchess, his manservant Bunter (who owed a good deal to Jeeves, we may think), his friend Freddie Arbuthnot, Inspector Parker and Sir Impey Biggs. Harriet Vane was not to appear until 1930 in *Strong Poison*, but we may consider that no collaboration was needed in the sketching of that idealistic character of Miss Sayers herself.

A second thought of the textual critic must be that Miss Sayers' narrative power, as exemplified in (say) the account of the Fenland flood in *The Nine Tailors* (London, 1934) was matched by her ability to write sparkling and convincing dialogue of the very highest order, a combination not achieved by every successful writer by any means. This second gift is amply demonstrated in (say) *The Devil to Pay* (Canterbury, 1939) and *The Man Born to be King* (London, 1943). These examples are apposite and deliberately chosen, since it is not suggested by Mrs Shreurs that Captain Fleming played any part in Miss Sayers' literary work other than the Wimsey stories. The point is therefore established that Miss Sayers could write excellent dialogue herself, without any help from anybody.

On the question of dates, discussed in the penultimate paragraph, Mrs Schreurs suggests by implication under the heading *1920s* AND RE-MARRIAGE that her father worked for Bensons, and that 'my father must have met Dorothy as soon as she went to Benson's, possibly before'. At that time Fleming had not lived with his wife and the family since the First World War, his divorce taking place in 1925. The fact of the matter is that we do not know when and in what circumstances Miss Sayers and Fleming first met. The remark of Mrs Schreurs is not supported by a recorded statement made by Lt-Col. R. L. Clarke, the Chairman of the Dorothy L. Sayers Historical and Literary Society, at a meeting of the Society held on 28 February, 1977. He said of Fleming:

> We know that he was definitely in the advertising world, and that he went into advertising after the war. Whether he went into Bensons we do not know; we have tried to find out, but all the Benson records have been destroyed. They cannot tell us much about Dorothy, let alone Fleming.

There is one piece of indirect evidence which should be quoted in fairness to Mrs Schreurs, since on the face of it it suggests that during the years before *Whose Body?* was published Miss Sayers may not have been averse to collaboration. At Oxford she became infatuated with Mr Eric Whelpton. He did not return her affections, since he was in love with someone else. In a long article by Miss Eve Sweeting, 'Is this Man the real Lord Peter Wimsey?', published in the *Braintree and Witham Times* of 17 June 1976, an interview with Mr Whelpton, now in his eighties and living at Rye in Sussex, was described. He and Miss Sayers remained on friendly terms after the war, and in the article he is quoted as saying:

> She asked me to go into partnership with her in writing crime books, as she and several of her friends were deliberately setting about to create a vogue for detective novels. I refused because I have no liking for that sort of thing, and I also expressed my belief that the public would not fall for anything so sordid. I was wrong, as I so often have been, but I do not regret my decision. She used to say that if I would collaborate with her, she would make me famous.

In her statement in support of her father Mrs Schreurs wrote: 'When I was small, we had a book called *How to See the Battlefields*. It had maps and diagrams—I remember it as having been written by my father. I may be wrong, but otherwise I cannot imagine why I should remember it at all.' Mrs Schreurs does not possess a copy of *How to See the Battlefields*, as she makes clear. It is a very scarce book indeed, and I will describe it in view of its rarity and the light it throws on the character of Fleming as he was in his thirties. The book is a crown 8vo, 7″ by 4½″, 124 pages in length, and was published by Cassell in September 1919, with the following title:

HOW TO SEE THE BATTLEFIELDS

by

CAPT. ATHERTON FLEMING

'Daily Chronicle' Special Correspondent, (1914)

With Fourteen Maps

CASSELL AND COMPANY, LTD.

London, New York, Toronto and Melbourne
1919

The Foreword describes the book as 'an endeavour, and a very crude one, to set before the public, in as concise a manner as possible, a certain amount of information which has been collected in the course of over four years of campaigning in France and Flanders'. It has at the foot the place and date of the Foreword: Wiston, July 1919, which we may presume to be Wiston in Lanarkshire, the county where Fleming's ashes were scattered after his death at his request.

The battlefields are dealt with in seven sections:

1. Nieuport—Ypres—Bailleul

2. Armentières—Bethune—Arras

3. The Somme and Cambrai

4. St. Quentin—Roye—Noyon

5. Montdidier—Compiègne—Soissons

6. The Retreat from Mons

7. From the Chemin-des-Dames to the Marne, 1918

As a war-correspondent in 1914 Fleming visited Arras, Bouchoire, Roye and Soissons. 'It was from one of the top windows of the Café des Voyageurs that I saw the first shell land in Arras in 1914.' Arras first fell into German hands on 15

September 1914. They only remained for a few days, and then bombarded the town. 'The first shell landed in Arras on October 6th, 1914, at five minutes past nine in the morning. This was the beginning of a deliberate bombardment of the *quartier* of the Hotel de Ville' (pp. 28–30).

On 7 May 1915, Fleming joined the Army Service Corps. He was apparently for a time at St. Omer, for he tells us that in the barracks there was stationed 'the A.S.C.(M.T.) School of Instruction, where a very large number of rankers received their course before taking a commission, and were licked into shape by one Captain Jarred, aided by a pocket-book containing all the latest stories, again aided by an absolutely unique knowledge of where to dine, wine or be entertained'.

Early in 1916 Fleming (now presumably commissioned) was posted to the Carency sector, where there had been heavy fighting in May 1915 and there were many exposed corpses:

> To this place, when the British took over that sector, came various howitzer batteries, and as the early part of 1916 was quite warm and spring-like, I can assure my readers, as one who arrived in the Carency sector attached to a certain 8-inch battery, that the place was little better than a huge cess-pit. Never have I seen such rats, or such numbers of them, as there were in the Carency sector. The place was literally alive with them; the only thing they could not manage to penetrate was corrugated iron. The only part of one's kit that was safe was the shrapnel-helmet, and I verily believe they tried to eat the paint off that.

In 1916 Fleming's brother was killed during the First Battle of the Somme, and was buried near Pozières. Fleming was on the Somme sector in October 1916. October—.

> . . . just when another two or three weeks of fine weather would have made all the difference in the world, was about the wettest and worst month for that time of the year that I can remember. Roads vanished under a sea of mud, guns got bogged down when they were moved up into position, ammunition lorries got stuck, and ammunition—heavy stuff, 8-inch and 9.2—had to be man-handled in order to keep the howitzers supplied.
>
> October was one long nightmare to anybody unfortunate enough to be in the Somme area. Many and many a time did we pray that our particular lot would be sent up to the comparative comfort of the

'Salient' at Ypres. I wonder if my readers remember the road to Hebuterne? That road broke the heart of more than one man on the ammunition supply. How the batteries ever got ammunition at all beats me hollow. And yet there are people who still think that the A.S.C.(M.T.) had a soft job!

Some of them had, no doubt, at the bases, but what about the poor devils who—many times—worked forty-eight hours on end, at least half the time under shell-fire, plunging and wallowing in and out of shell-holes, lorries heavily laden with shells and cartridges, well over the axles in mud, no lights, and very often no food, and not the slightest protection in the way of trench or dug-out when the road was under fire? And yet, in spite of it all, the guns were fed and the shells arrived at the batteries somehow or other! When looking at these roads and tracks in the Somme area—roads up to the battery positions—try to imagine what it must have been like to work without lights at night—battery positions cannot be reached in the daytime except on certain occasions—and when the least error of judgment or sleepiness on the part of the drivers might precipitate both lorry and contents into some huge shell-hole or mine crater. The job of the driver on a heavy ammunition lorry was no sinecure, and the gunners themselves—to do them justice—are the first to admit it.

Fleming appears to have been in the Bailleul area during the Third Battle of Ypres, 1917. In March 1918 Fleming was involved in the withdrawal from the Ham–Guiscard–Noyon region. He was at Noyon with part of his unit, and received orders to retire to Montdidier. He had a considerable amount of material to move, and needing to know how far away the enemy was, he went out at night by car with an Australian officer. They found themselves in the British front line—'a thin line of tired-out men'—and he hastily returned to Noyon to complete the removal of the material to Montdidier.

Later he was concerned in the withdrawal from the Chemin-des-Dames to the Marne, and his account of this operation is evidently based on first-hand experience. During the rearguard action certain regiments put up 'a very stubborn resistance, and were the means of saving several heavy guns by holding up the enemy long enough for the gunners and the Army Service Corps to get them on the move—hauled by the huge caterpillar tractors, whose maximum speed is about two and a half miles per hour. For these caterpillar drivers I have the greatest admiration; they would drive through anything, and on more than one occasion they have been attacked by the enemy and have beaten him off.'

In 1976 I loaned *How to See the Battlefields* to Mrs Sheila Paton Smith of Clevelands, Felsted, Essex. Mrs Paton Smith (formerly Miss Dorothy Lake) had been Miss Sayers' secretary from the early nineteen-thirties to the outbreak of the Second World War, a period when Miss Sayers and her husband were living mainly in Witham. In her letter to me of 2 September 1976 Mrs Paton Smith wrote:

> I finished the book on Tuesday evening, and return it to you with my thanks. It is good straightforward stuff, and is typical of Mac Fleming as he was when I knew him.

My friend C. Wilfrid Scott-Giles also read the book, and sent me his impression of it in his letter of 10 August 1976:

> It was, of course, no part of the book to detail his own career, but from certain personal experiences we learn that he was concerned with the supply of heavy ammunition to the gunners, and while seldom in the front line he was often under fire behind the lines. He was at Carency in May 1916, on the Somme sector in October 1916, at Bailleul in 1917 (the third battle of Ypres) and the withdrawal to the Marne in 1918.
>
> He reached the permanent rank of Captain, but probably had the acting rank of Major, since later in life he was sometimes known as Major Fleming. It was a good, sound record, typical of so many of my contemporaries who served in the first World War, and received (as Fleming did) no honours but 'Mutt and Jeff' and the Victory Medal.
>
> You will notice that the Foreword indicates that the book was written at Wiston—presumably Lanarkshire—so Fleming appears not to have been living with his family when he wrote it. His daughter, Ann Schreurs, says he rarely visited his family after the war. . . . In some ways he may have been an unsatisfactory person, but his book leaves me with a favourable impression of the man behind it, and I think the good in his record should be made public.

I agree with Wilfrid Scott-Giles in these generous sentiments, and believe that the picture of Fleming that emerges from his unpretentious book is that of a good soldier who endured a hard war. I have thought it right to present, within the obvious limitations of space, a reasonable impression of an honest book, sometimes in the author's own words, which few Sayers students of today seem to have read, because of its scarcity. Although apparently physically unscathed by his military service, apart from the possible after effects of gas mentioned by some who knew him in Witham, it seems entirely possible that Fleming suffered in other ways. I refer to the kind of psychological strain so vividly described by Miss Sayers in *The Unpleasantness at the Bellona Club* (London, 1928) in her picture of Captain George Fentiman, a disillusioned ex-officer who found it impossible to adjust himself adequately to civilian life in post-war England after his experiences in the European conflict. Miss Sayers wrote on pages 21–2 of that book that Wimsey knew better than Mr Murbles 'the kind of mental and physical strain George Fentiman had undergone. The War pressed hardly upon imaginative men in responsible positions.'[1] I have sometimes wondered whether the character of Fentiman was based, to some extent at least, on that of Fleming. There must have been some reason for the latter's post-war behaviour towards his first wife and two daughters, whom he seldom visited and did not support, according to the statement of Mrs Schruers. It is significant, perhaps, in our judgment of Fleming, that this document shows that Mrs Schreurs' memory of her father today, despite all that occurred, is still one of admiration and affection.

Mrs Hitchman tells us on page 71 of *Such a Strange Lady* that Fleming was christened Oswald Arthur, which he changed to Oswold Atherton. In such documents as I have seen he does not seem to have made any use of 'Oswold', but he was certainly known as 'Atherton Fleming'. He married Miss Sayers under this name, in which she certainly acquiesced, for she used 'Atherton' as her husband's single forename in her entries in *Who's Who*.

Previous commentators appear to be united in their view that the disadvantages of the marriage were wholly borne by Miss Sayers. Mrs Hitchman tells us on page 73 of her book that it was 'Dorothy who provided the home and paid the bills. Oswold left

---

[1] Wimsey's nightmares of his own war-time experiences are relevant.

his place in Hammersmith and joined her in Great James Street.'
She continues:

> The fiction was kept up for a year or two that he was a journalist
> 'and not always master of his time' as Dorothy wrote when accepting
> a luncheon invitation. In spite of diligent search I have not been able
> to find anything under his name. He is supposed to have been a
> motoring correspondent for the *News of the World*, and to have
> written a cookery column as 'Gourmet' for the *Evening News*, but
> both these papers disown him. He did produce a cookery book at
> some time, but it is suspected that his 'journalism' may have
> consisted mostly of propping up well known Fleet Street bars.

David Higham, Miss Sayers' literary agent, writing on page
211 of his autobiography *Literary Gent* (London 1978) of the
period after she had ceased to work for Bensons in 1930, seems
to have shared Mrs Hitchman's opinion of Fleming:

> From then on, freed from her copywriting stint, she could go
> forward, and did, undefeated by a marriage which turned out to be
> disastrous. She had taken on Mac, her husband, at least partly, I
> think, because she thought she might cure his drinking—a hopeless
> task she never should even have thought of. Quite late in her life with
> him—she was no believer in divorce—she told me how he would nag
> her to her desk if, himself completely idle and comfortable on the
> bottles she earned for him, he thought she was neglecting it. She had
> weathered many years of this, and was rewarded with a success as
> solid as she could wish: Mac could and did have as many bottles as
> he liked until he died, leaving her to a reasonable stretch of peace-
> ful widowhood.

These strictures are severe, and do not carry complete
conviction. A letter from Miss Sayers to a friend in 1928 and
quoted in part by Mrs Hitchman on pages 73–4 of her book
suggests that she was happy in the early years of her marriage at
least. The flat in Great James Street was being enlarged and
altered, and Miss Sayers wrote:

> My husband is giving his celebrated impersonation of the Mayor
> and Corporation of Ypres surveying the ruins of the Cloth Hall. I
> am trying to look like Dido rebuilding Carthage, and hoping (as I
> daresay she did) that the hammering will soon be over.
> Life is very wonderful.

This was not the letter of a discontented woman. Miss Muriel St Clare Byrne, Miss Sayers' closest friend, has said that Mac could be very charming, and that she never had seen him drunk. He was a clever artist in oils and crayon, and both Miss Byrne and Mrs Paton Smith possess excellent paintings in oils by Fleming, which they are proud to own and display. Both are signed 'Pigalle'. In the same year as that of the letter quoted above, 1928, Miss St Clare Byrne recalls having supper with the Flemings at Great James Street. The meal was prepared by Dorothy, who was skilled in cooking. The couple were gay and happy, but not demonstrably affectionate. Fleming was on good terms with his wife's other two close friends, Helen Simpson and Norah Lambourne who, with Muriel St Clare Byrne, often came to stay at Witham when the Flemings bought their house there. Mrs Paton Smith has said that during her period as Miss Sayers' secretary she never heard them quarrelling.

On the other hand, Miss Muriel St Clare Byrne has recorded that after the first few years, and especially during the later period when the Flemings lived mainly in Witham, they began to irritate each other. Notes taken of an interview with Miss Byrne by Lt-Col. R. L. Clarke on 22 August 1976 include the following:

> There was no question of any other woman being the cause of conflict between them; they just got on each other's nerves. Mac did not at that time drink to excess. . . . Nevertheless, they cared for each other in a way. Mac loved Dorothy but realised that he upset her. He was in tears one day when he said to Muriel St. Clare Byrne, 'What can I do to please her? She doesn't think I love her, but I do. Nothing I do seems to make any difference'.

By contrast, however, Miss Byrne said that Dorothy often talked of Mac with pride, and often mentioned his cookery book, of which I shall have more to say. Mac spoke with pride of Dorothy, but never discussed her work. There was no sign of any literary collaboration between them, but Miss Byrne believes that Dorothy drew on Mac's knowledge of cars, painting and photography for some of the technical details in her books. There is some independent evidence for this opinion from Colonel John Taylor, whom I have quoted elsewhere in this book.

Mrs. Sheila Paton Smith said that during her period as Miss Sayers' secretary the Flemings did not go out together in Witham. Dorothy had the front room on the first floor as her library where she wrote, and Mac had a small room downstairs where he drew or painted. They had separate bedrooms. They met for lunch and dinner, but as Dorothy's habit was to work after dinner into the small hours, rising very late, they spent little time together. She thought that any literary collaboration was extremely unlikely in these circumstances. Mrs Paton Smith was kind enough to lend me a book presented to her by Fleming, *The Craft of the Short Story* (Pitman, 1936), by Donald Maconochie, which he said he had written himself under this *nom de plume*, and of which I shall have more to say in due course.

Miss Kathleen Richards became Miss Sayers' part-time secretary when Mrs Paton Smith had to leave at the outbreak of the Second World War. She has a vivid recollection of her employer's beautiful speaking voice, and of her habit of working far into the night. Her opinion of Miss Sayers was that she was quite the most brillliant person one could ever hope to meet. She did not see much of Fleming, apart from occasional chats. He was a regular customer of the Red Lion in Witham. Miss Richards doubted the originality of his cookery book. She was the principal speaker at a meeting of the Dorothy L. Sayers Historical and Literary Society held in Witham on 28 February, 1977, which was recorded on tape. Miss Richards remarked of Fleming:

> I never had the impression from what I knew of him that he had a great deal of talent. I assume that if he did any writing, he did not do it after they were married. I think he just did his crayon drawings, and had a very leisurely life. This is what I think would have upset Miss Sayers. One has to remember that she made her own way, and to my mind there is no doubt that she was the bread winner. . . . I can quite see why they did fall out, although I did not personally ever hear them quarrelling. The only time I heard much of them was when there were people staying in the house, when it was all very jolly—and to me slightly false.

To my mind the problems of the marriage arose principally from the fact that Fleming was a likeable, ordinary man, who had been a journalist and had written his book *How to See the Battlefields* in 1919 after suffering at least psychologically from a long hard war. He had married a brilliant woman with a circle of Oxford friends, with educational and family backgrounds somewhat different from his own. They were, moreover, all involved in literary work of one sort or another, as he had been in a very different sphere, a fact of which he was doubtless acutely aware. He had his weaknesses, as we all have, and one seems to have been the more congenial atmosphere of the Red Lion. Even this was spoilt for him on one occasion at least, as Miss Richards revealed in one of her remarks during the meeting, possibly without realising its extreme significance. 'There is a story that he went into the Red Lion once, and somebody said, "This is Dorothy Sayers' husband." He stubbed out his cigarette and walked out.'

The story of the cookery book is of great interest, for in my opinion it tells us a great deal about Fleming. Since, moreover, Mrs Hitchman's reference to it is limited to the phrase, quoted elsewhere in this book, that Fleming 'did produce a cookery book at some time', a somewhat more precise account of the book would seem to be appropriate. I read the book in company with my friend Ralph Clarke on the occasion of my first visit to Witham in the autumn of 1976. We were able to borrow it from its present owner, to whom it had been presented by Fleming. The title-page, which bears the written inscription 'To F. W. East, With the Author's Compliments', reads:

GOURMET'S

BOOK OF FOOD
AND DRINK

With Decorations in Colour
by HENDY

LONDON
John Lane. The Bodley Head, London.

It was published in 1933. It consists of xiv + 278 pages, with amusing coloured line drawings, and is dedicated 'To my wife.

Who can make an Omelette.' The book has no entry in Fleming's name in the *British Museum General Catalogue of Printed Books*, so that my first step was to try to obtain such information about the author as might be available from the publishers. I accordingly wrote to Mr Max Reinhardt, the Managing Director of The Bodley Head, who was kind enough to write to me personally to say that the firm's contract files recorded the author as Captain Atherton Fleming.

The literary style of the book is entirely different from that of *How to See the Battlefields*. In the Foreword 'Gourmet' insists that 'this book is *not* a cookery book', although it does contain a large number of recipes, 'which from time to time have appealed to my own palate and to those of my gourmet friends'. The book is pretentiously written and vaguely autobiographical in style, in that the text is enlivened by anecdotes of the author's experiences in connexion with food and drink in many countries, often in expensive surroundings and in distinguished company. Few of these stories appear to coincide with what we know of Fleming. Thus on page 40 he discusses the excellence of the steak and potato pie he used to eat in his youth in Norfolk. If Fleming, born in Kirkwall, spent any part of his early life in Norfolk, it is not mentioned by his daughter in her account of the family history. Be that as it may, the author makes clear that in adult life his eating habits extended beyond Norfolk steak and potato pie. On page 34, discussing the one-minute steak, he remarks that 'The grill chef at the Savoy has produced some very fine examples'.

At the foot of the same page, after a general criticism of the gastronomical tastes of 'the fair sex', including what Fleming regarded as their partiality to chicken, ices of the Pêche Melba type, sweet wines of all varieties, and any kind of liqueur with a pretty colour, the author tells the following story, which extends to page 35 and is a useful example of the kind of anecdote with which the book abounds. It makes amusing reading, but leaves us in no doubt that the author intends us to believe that he moved in wealthy circles and surroundings:

> There are exceptions, of course, to every rule. I well remember one dear old lady who although on the shady side of sixty made periodic visits to Town principally—so she confided to me—for the

purpose of going to Simpson's in the Strand and tucking into turbot and roast saddle of mutton, which was invariably accompanied by a pint tankard of Bass's No. 1 and bitter beer mixed. A very delightful woman indeed, a fine judge of a horse, and one of the straightest riders to hounds one could wish to see. I took her to lunch at a fashionable London restaurant one day where she promptly confounded the head waiter by telling him to 'cut out all the à la's', that she would begin with a 'a dozen Whitstable natives, after that game pie with plenty of jelly, Stilton and a pint of stout'—to all of which she did full justice.

The author makes it clear on page 75 that he is very familiar with Simpson's himself:

I know of but one place in London where roast beef and roast mutton are cooked, and served, in perfection, and that is Simpson's in the Strand. Simpson's is more than a mere restaurant, it is an institution.

Despite his choice of the best places to eat both at home and abroad (the author tells us on page 72, for example, 'Vol-au-vent à la Normande I was once privileged to taste in perfection at the principal hotel in Verneuil'), he is on occasions unreservedly critical, as is exemplified on pages 24–5:

I have been served with poisonously bad coffee in more than one of the best Paris hotels. The same misfortune has happened to me on several occasions in *most* expensive London palaces.

In my opinion, one of the most pretentious pieces of writing in the book appears on pages 48–9:

In the days before the War there used to be a little club of gourmets of whom the late John Hollingshead was one of our members, who crossed every Sunday morning to Calais, lunched at the buffet and came back by an afternoon boat, obtaining on their outing a fine brisk-up of sea air and an excellent luncheon, for the Calais buffet was, and still is, famous for the quality of its victuals and wines. As an alternative, why not motor to Folkestone, cross to Boulogne, lunch at the Meurice, or the Chrystol, look in for an hour at the Casino and get back to Town for dinner.

To be thoroughly modern, the correct thing to do is to have a 'flip' over to Le Touquet, or Paris Plage, or even further afield to Paris. Paris on a Sunday is at its best, and on a sunny day in spring or autumn to sit down to a perfectly chosen and cooked déjeuner in one of the more fashionable restaurants is to see *tout Paris* and thoroughly enjoy life.

The geographical ramifications of the book are wide indeed. On page 86 the author expresses his appreciation of 'the highest branches of Teutonic cookery, which successfully rival the *haute cuisine* of the French', exemplified by his enjoyment of *Boullabaisse à la Provençale* in the Mediterranean resorts. On page 53 he closes a chapter with the following:

> I am writing of the Hawaiian Islands as I knew them thirty years ago—long before Hollywood took them over—one of these days, please God, I shall return, just to see what damage the so-called modern civilisation has caused.

On page 15 the author is critical of American chefs, but is complimentary on page 17 as regards breakfast served in 'any reputable American hotel'. He adds:

> The American breakfast is no small thing, if one can judge by the staggering assortment of mixed eatables which appeared on a certain New York hotel menu I well remember. There were at least one hundred dishes to choose from, and the general 'get up' of this wonderful card reminded me more of an illuminated address than a bill of fare.

We may wonder how the details of the American hotel menu compared with that of the breakfast bill-of-fare on the *Mauretania*, where on page 183 the author tells us he was in May 1931:

> Seven-thirty a.m. Two days out from England, en route for New York, gorgeous weather, and the sea like the proverbial mill-pond. A quarter of an hour in the gym, a swim in the swimming pool, dress and, with a sailor's hunger, breakfast. Breakfast aboard a Cunarder on the high seas is one of the most delightful meals of the day, there are so many nice things to eat—or at any rate to choose from—and the sea air strops up the appetite to such a keen edge that even non-breakfasters are tempted and fall.

According to everyone I have met who knew Miss Sayers, and to the immense mass of printed material about her assiduously collected and preserved in the archives of the Dorothy L. Sayers Historical and Literary Society at Witham, there is no record of either her or her husband ever having visited America. I therefore think that the *Mauretania* story is pure fiction, and I include in that criticism most of the autobiographical asides included in the text of *Gourmet's Book of Food and Drink*. I believe this to be the reason why Fleming wrote it anonymously. He had published one book in his own name in 1919 as we know, and another satisfactory and interesting volume with his name on the title-page would have increased such literary reputation as he possessed. Why then the anonymity? The *Mauretania* story is a useful example of the answer. The book was published in 1933, and there must have been many friends and acquaintances in Witham (in the Red Lion, for example) who could remember whether or not he sailed to America in 1931.

Fleming seems to have been an attractive but somewhat inadequate person following his participation in the First World War, overshadowed by his brilliant wife's accomplishments but content to be financially dependent upon her, yet at the same time resentful of his embarrassing situation as 'Miss Sayers' husband'. It seems to me possible that the pretentious, anecdotal portions of his book represented his daydreams of the type of man he would have liked to have been—wealthy, independent, widely travelled and socially accomplished. Doubtless the practical motive for writing the book was money, and in this he may have been encouraged by his wife. Miss Muriel St Clare Byrne has said that when she and Miss Sayers went on a motoring holiday together, the latter insisted upon stopping at book shops to enquire if *Gourmet's Book of Food and Drink* was in stock.

In the *Foreword* the author said that for many years he had made a hobby of collecting cookery books of all kinds. If this was true, then the provenance of the recipes included in *Gourmet's Book of Food and Drink* does not present a problem. Two at least of the recipes, 'Ham in Hades' and 'Alderman's Walk', respectively printed on pages 41–2 and 43, are closely copied from the *Recipe-Book of the Mustard Club* (pages 10 and 14),[1] a booklet which formed part of the very successful advertising campaign designed for J. & J. Colman of Norwich in the late 1920s. A good deal of the phraseology is exact. Miss Sayers

[1] See the Appendix to this chapter.

worked for Benson's, the agents concerned, at this period, and while there is no evidence available that she was engaged on the actual Mustard Club campaign, there is no reason to suppose that a copy of the *Recipe-Book* would not be available in the Fleming household.

I have wondered a little about Mrs Hitchman's remark on page 73 of her book, already quoted by me in another context, that Fleming was 'supposed' to have written a cookery column as 'Gourmet' for the *Evening News*, but that in response to her inquiries that paper disowned knowledge of him. I do not doubt Mrs Hitchman's account, but it is odd that on the page following the title of *Gourmet's Book of Food and Drink* there is an acknowledgment 'To the Editor of the *Evening News*, for permission to quote from certain articles of mine which were exclusive to that journal'. If Fleming did write cookery articles for the *Evening News*, and used the texts *verbatim* in his book, it would explain why there are so many references to a man cooking for himself in 'a bachelor establishment', on the assumption that the articles were written before his marriage to Miss Sayers, and during the period from the end of the war when he was separated from his first wife Winifred. Thus on page 22 he writes: 'In a bachelor establishment there are few cookery utensils more useful than the chafing-dish. . . . Breakfast prepared by oneself in a chafing-dish is an enjoyable meal'. He adds that any breakfast dish 'is at the disposal of the self-contained bachelor who is the possessor of a chafer'. On page 48 he writes: 'To the lonely bachelor, luncheon in London on a Sunday is usually a ghastly meal.' On the third page of the book he remarks that 'as nobody seems inclined to look after Number One he will be well advised to have a shot at looking after himself'. These are curious expressions coming from an author who had been married for seven years when his book was published, and dedicated it to his wife.

When I was in Witham in 1976 Mrs Sheila Paton Smith most kindly loaned me a copy of a book I have never seen either before or since. It is *The Craft of the Short Story* by Donald Maconochie, published by Sir Isaac Pitman and Sons, Ltd in 1936. Mrs Paton Smith told me that about 1936, when she was Miss Sayers' part-time secretary, and the Flemings were living mainly in Witham, Captain Fleming gave her the book. He said he was the author, and that he wished her to have a copy as a present. The book bears no inscription, and at some time the fly-leaf (the front free end-paper) has been removed. In all other aspects the book is a fine copy in its original wrappers. Mrs Paton Smith has no recollection of the missing fly-leaf, and told me that she had not noticed its absence until I pointed it out.

As Maconochie was the maiden name of Fleming's mother, it seemed possible that 'Donald Maconochie' was a pseudonym used by him instead of his own name on the title-page, although the reason, whatever it was, seemed just as mysterious to me as in the case of *Gourmet's Book of Food and Drink*. However, the thing to do was to ascertain the facts, if this was possible. I accordingly wrote to the publishers, who replied promptly and courteously enclosing a xerox of the Agreement. It was dated 29 January 1936 and was signed 'Donald Maconochie' in a flowing hand. It was witnessed by 'Dorothy L. Fleming, 24 Newland Street, Witham, Essex', which seemed to me to settle the matter of the identity of 'Donald Maconochie' as Atherton Fleming.

The book is a very short one, consisting of viii + 96 pages + 32 pages of advertisements of other Pitman publications. The text is actually 88 pages, since 8 pages (82–9) are occupied by addresses and details of 44 magazines published in 1936 who were possible printers of short stories. In the preface the author said that he had been a writer for thirty years, in the capacities of editor, short story writer and the author of published books, and that he could 'look back with quiet satisfaction on the past years as not being altogether ill-spent'. He added that he had 'had to earn his bread and butter by writing' and that Fate had 'not been unkind'. He said that the object of the book was to help 'the budding writer, and be able, by means of hints and tips I have collected together in the following pages, to help him—or her— to steer clear of that yawning cavern, the waste paper basket.' The most astonishing piece of advice contained in a book published pseudonymously appears on page 80, and is that one should never write under a *nom de plume*. 'Personally, I think that an author is well advised to use his or her name fearlessly. Incidentally, there is less fear of errors in book-keeping at the office of the magazine.'

The book has eight short chapters, 'The Approach to the Short Story', 'The Principles of Good Technique', 'Characterisation', 'The Plot and Type of Story', 'Literary Style', 'The Dialogue and the Setting', 'The Writing of the Story', and 'How to sell the Story'. I cannot offer a professional opinion of the quality of the advice contained in *The Craft of the Short Story*, for I have never written any fiction myself. It does seem to me, however, that this short book contains a certain amount of information that may be considered superfluous to the needs of the writer of short stories. On pages 79–80, for example, he suggests it is a mistake to submit a manuscript that 'is not typewritten but is written in ink with various corrections on sheets of paper of different sizes'. He advises the writer who does not possess a typewriter 'to take his work to a typewriting office and have it neatly typed at a cost of a shilling per thousand words', and in time 'buy a typewriter for himself with the money earned by his literary efforts'. Fleming advises that on the first page of the manuscript should 'appear the title, author's name and number of words, and a very brief synopsis of the story'. His example of a synopsis for the guidance of the reader follows:

CROSS CURRENTS

by

Arnold Rogers

A Modern Story in which the
Conflicting Interests of the
Main Characters Lead to Tense
and Dramatic Scenes—and to
a Remarkable Climax

Fleming adds (page 81) that manuscripts should be only typed on one side of the paper.

Two pages of the short chapter on 'The Dialogue and the Setting' are reproduced from essays on these subjects respectively written by Anthony Trollope and Robert Louis Stevenson, but I think it unfortunate that the reader is not given the references of the sources of these valuable paragraphs. Fleming seems to have been familiar with the work of both Trollope and Stevenson, and with that of Bret Harte, O. Henry, W. W. Jacobs, Sir Arthur Quiller-Couch, Guy de Maupassant and Eden Phillpots. Possibly significantly, however, he writes on page 43 that the detective story is the most popular short literary form, and devotes four pages of the short chapter on 'The Plot and the Type of Story' to the work of Sir Arthur Conan Doyle. Fleming shows his familiarity with the stories of Wilkie Collins, G. K. Chesterton, Edgar Allan Poe and even those about Sexton Blake. The work of Dorothy L. Sayers is not mentioned, but it is difficult to avoid the impression that she may have been the source of some of the information.

I do not know what experience in the writing of short stories Fleming drew upon to enable him to put this short book together, for I have not so far been able to trace in the resources of a very large library with which I happen to be connected any story by Atherton Fleming or Donald Maconochie. He does not, however, refrain from indulging in literary criticism of the work of unnamed persons who have failed to share his own good fortune in making his living as a writer for 'over thirty years', a period on which he can 'look back with quiet satisfaction'. On page 91 he tells us why some writers' work is not accepted for publication:

> The authors have begun their story without any idea—or at the most a very hazy idea—of how they are going to continue it. They have meandered on, added ordinary incidents and dull conversations to the story, and have attempted an ending like something they have read. The whole effort is formless, pointless and ineffective.

It will be seen from this essay that in my opinion Fleming wrote one good book, *How to See the Battlefields*, a straightforward account of his experiences as a serving officer in France and Flanders during the First World War. It is perhaps significant that he put his own name on the title-page, thus following the advice he gave in *The Craft of the Short Story* written 17 years later under a pseudonym. It seems ironic that he appears to have gained no literary advantage by his marriage to Dorothy L. Sayers, and simply became in the eyes of his acquaintances 'Miss Sayers' husband.' On the evidence of his second and third books, my opinion is that he did not possess the literary skill or originality to offer any useful collaboration in the writing of the Wimsey stories. At most, I believe that he was at times able to assist his wife by providing information on minor matters that had come within his personal experience.

APPENDIX
A COMPARISON OF TEXTS

GOURMET'S BOOK OF FOOD AND DRINK	THE RECIPE-BOOK OF THE MUSTARD CLUB
Alderman's Walk, p. 43	*Alderman's Walk*, p. 14

Number One will be well advised to pay some little attention to the food he consumes by considering the merits of one of the oldest of English delicacies, *Alderman's Walk*. This dish is prepared from the most exquisite portion of the most exquisite joint in Cookerydom, and is so called because in olden times at City dinners it is alleged to gave been reserved for the Aldermen. It is none other than the first, longest and juiciest longitudinal slice, next to the bone, of a succulent saddle of mutton, Southdown for choice, and of somewhat mature age, four years if possible. Tenderly, and with due reverence, this slice is removed from the hot joint, sizzling from the oven; it is then laid aside on a slice of bread cut to its own length, whereon it is let grow cold; thoroughly cold. Prepare then, in a chafing-dish, a sauce composed of a walnut of butter, three drops of Tabasco, three chopped chives, and an egg-spoonful of made mustard. Stir these ingredients until the amalga-

Alderman's Walk is a very old English delicacy, the most exquisite portion of the most exquisite joint in Cookerydom, and so called because at City dinners in our grandfathers' times it is alleged to have been reserved for the Aldermen. It is composed of the first, longest and juiciest longitudinal slice, next to the bone, of a succulent saddle of mutton—Southdown for choice, and four years old at that. Remove this slice tenderly, lay it aside on a slice of bread its own length, and let it grow thoroughly cold. Prepare then a sauce composed of a walnut of butter, a teaspoonful of Worcester, three drops of tabasco, three chopped chives, and a small teaspoonful of made Mustard. Stir these ingredients in a sauce-pan until quite smooth. Then take the bread, which should have absorbed a good deal of juice from the Alderman's Walk, cut into strips, and lightly toast. Drop the meat into the sauce, and let it cook for eight minutes, turning it once.

GOURMET'S BOOK OF FOOD
AND DRINK

mation is smooth and complete. Then take the bread, which should have a good deal of juice from under the Alderman's Walk, cut into strips, and lightly toast the strips. Drop the meat into the sauce, and let it cook for eight minutes, turning it once—that is four minutes for each side. Slide it out on a hot dish, put the toast around it, eat it quickly and then, in silent meditation, give Thanks.

Ham in Hades, pp. 41–2

Ham in Hades as a luncheon, or breakfast, dish is good. To the jaded palate it has a caressing tang that tints the morning mists with a rosy blush, and turns the laziest man into a 'go-getter'. It is a dangerous dish to place before a hungry fellow! This is the way to Hades your Ham:

Make a mixture of a teaspoonful of made mustard, a tablespoonful of Tarragon vinegar, a pinch of salt, a teaspoonful of paprika and a teaspoonful of Worcester Sauce. Spread this mixture on both sides of, say, half a dozen slices of ham. Put two tablespoonfuls of pure olive oil into a frying pan (or you can cook the whole doings in a chafing-dish on the sideboard). When this begins to smoke, put in the ham and brown it quickly on both sides—five minutes will be ample. Particularly note that this dish is neither hot nor oily, though it sounds both."

THE RECIPE-BOOK OF THE
MUSTARD CLUB

Slide it out on a hot dish, put the toast around it, eat it in a hurry, and thank your stars you are alive to enjoy it.

Ham in Hades, p. 10

Here is a breakfast dish that will send hubby to town feeling like two men. It is worth one new hat at least, if only because it makes a break in the ever-lasting cycle of bacon and eggs—and this how to Hades your Ham.

Make a mixture of a teaspoonful of made Mustard, a tablespoonful of tarragon vinegar, pinch of salt, teaspoonful of paprika and a teaspoonful of Worcester Sauce. Spread this mixture on both sides of half a dozen slices of cooked ham. Put two tablespoonfuls of olive oil in the frying pan, and when this begins to smoke, put in the ham and brown it quickly on both sides. Sounds hot and oily, but it is neither one nor t'other, but it is very *moreish*.

VI

THE DOCUMENTS IN THE CASE

In the archives of the Dorothy L. Sayers Historical and Literary Society at Witham in Essex is a bound 363-page typescript entitled *Dorothy Sayers: Novelist*, by Sara Lee Soloway of the University of Kentucky, Lexington, Kentucky. It is dated 1971 and the sub-title reads: 'A dissertation submitted in partial fulfilment of the requirements for the degree of Doctor of Philosophy at the University of Kentucky'. It is a thoughtful piece of work, which I read with interest and pleasure. In my opinion, however, it is marred by two omissions, the first being in the title. Miss Sayers would have taken great exception to having the initial 'L', representing her mother's maiden name of Leigh, omitted from her name. As I have had occasion to point point out in Chapter III, her second English publisher, Ernest Benn, was reprimanded for the printing of her name as 'Dorothy Sayers' on the spine of the first edition of *The Unpleasantness at the Bellona Club* (London, 1928), which is before me as I write. It is of interest to compare the identically bound first edition of *The Documents in the Case* (London, 1930) published by Benn, which I am also fortunate enough to possess. The names of the collaborating authors are printed on the spine as 'Dorothy L. Sayers and Robert Eustace'.

The second omission in Ms Soloway's dissertation is a total lack of any discussion of *The Documents in the Case*. It does not appear in the 'Table of Contents. Dorothy Sayers: Novelist' on p. vi, which lists only the eleven full-length novels concerning Lord Peter Wimsey. In the text of the dissertation, moreover, no mention is made of the fact that in 1930 Miss Sayers published *The Documents in the Case* as well as *Strong Poison*. It is true that Ms Soloway appears to be predominantly interested in Lord Peter Wimsey and his later relationship with Harriet Vane, and indeed groups her treatment of the novels into 'Lord Peter Investigates' and 'The Harriet-Peter Novels'. Her indulgence in this preference, however, seems to me to be at variance with the inclusive title of the dissertation, *Dorothy Sayers: Novelist*, since in my view *The Documents in the Case* is one of the most interesting of her full-length detective stories, despite its lack of scientific accuracy, about which I shall have something to say. Its epistolary presentation, for example, follows that of Wilkie Collins' *The Moonstone*, which Miss Sayers regarded as 'probably the very finest detective story ever written'.[1] Her own use, therefore, in *The Documents in the Case*, of the similar device of telling the story by means of a series of letters and narratives from the pens of the various characters must be of the greatest interest to any student of the development of her literary work. On pages 33–6 of her Introduction to *Great Short Stories of Detection, Mystery and Horror*, moreover, Miss Sayers wrote with admiration of the skill of E. C. Bentley, the author of the classic *Trent's Last Case* (London, 1913) in his use of the shift of the different viewpoints of the characters in the story, a presentation which herself was able similarly to employ in *The Documents in the Case*, thanks to the framework of the novel. The opinion of Sara Lee Soloway on these matters would have added to the value of her doctoral thesis.

The Documents in the Case is the story of an illicit sexual liaison between Margaret, the second wife of an elderly engineer, George Harrison, who is twenty years older than herself, and an artist of her own age, Howard Lathom. Harrison, one of whose hobbies is the practical study and cooking of edible fungi, is murdered by Lathom, at least partly at the instigation of Mrs Harrison, who pretends that she has become pregnant by him. The crime is committed by the secret introduction of a quantity of synthetic muscarine, stolen by Lathom from a laboratory, into a dish of harmless edible fungi, gathered, cooked and eaten by

[1] *Great Short Stories of Detection, Mystery and Horror* (London, 1928), Edited by Dorothy L. Sayers, p. 25.

Harrison, thus successfully giving the impression that some poisonous fungi, similar in appearance to the innocent variety, containing natural, organic muscarine, had been collected by mistake.

On p. 75 of her *Such a Strange Lady* (London, 1975), Mrs Janet Hitchman says that *The Documents in the Case* is one of the most revealing of all Miss Sayers' novels. Mrs Hitchman contends that the character of George Harrison is based on that of Miss Sayers' husband, Atherton Fleming, and that the book was written as a calculated message to Fleming, 'not warning him that she might poison him, that is a bit too fanciful, but showing him how his attitude was poisoning their lives' (p. 76). Mrs Hitchman devotes three pages to her interpretation of the *fons et origo* of *The Documents in the Case*, which she seems to think probably failed in its purpose:

> It is doubtful if Fleming's shallow mind could take in the lessons she was trying to instil, he may not even have read her books, but at least she had unburdened herself, and showed how a marriage could be futilely worn away. (p. 77)

Mrs Hitchman impresses upon us what she regards as important similarities between Fleming and Miss Sayers' portrait of Harrison. Her principal points are that both were pedantic and pompous, that both claimed to be expert cooks and that Harrison bullied his wife and demanded her utmost obedience. She concedes that Fleming failed to bully Miss Sayers, but tells us that he tried to do so. I do not think that there is any acceptable evidence to support these contentions.

According to Mrs Hitchman herself (p. 73) Fleming was 'a weak "Bonnie Prince Charlie" type, looking for a cushy billet' when he married Miss Sayers, 'who provided the home and paid the bills'. His alleged 'journalism', Mrs Hitchman suspects, 'consisted mostly of propping up well known Fleet Street bars'. Harrison, on the other hand, was a diligent and responsible professional man. In a letter to Lathom of 6 June, 1929 (*The Documents in the Case*, p. 128) Margaret says of her husband, 'He thinks more of his firm than of anything else in the world— far more than he does of me or my happiness'.

One of the principal narrators in *The Documents in the Case* is the writer John Munting, who shares rooms in the Harrison's home in Bayswater with the artist Lathom. He tells a great part of the story in a series of letters to his fiancée, Elizabeth Drake. He is not involved in the developing and sinister situation between Lathom and the Harrisons, and for a time is unaware of the facts. His views, expressed in his letters, simply give an impartial account of life under the Harrison roof through the observant eyes of a professional writer. Early in the book (p. 25) he describes Mrs Harrison as 'a sort of suburban vamp' who has 'evidently got her husband by the short hairs'. Harrison is depicted as 'small, thin, rather stooping . . . [with] a decentish post of some kind with a firm of civil engineers'. In a letter quoted on p. 86 Munting adds, 'Harrison would cheerfully die for his wife . . . I like Harrison—I think he's worth a hundred of her'. On p. 45 he describes Mrs Harrison's mouth as 'sloppy and bad', and as early as p. 31 he writes with great insight, 'There's something wrong in this house—something more than a little misunderstanding about dinner time. I shouldn't wonder if she gives this man a devil of a time.'

This picture of George and Margaret Harrison and their marriage as depicted in *The Documents in the Case* bears little resemblance, we may think, to the relationship between Dorothy L. Sayers and her husband, *circa* 1930. I am fortunate in having a friend, Colonel John H. Taylor, C.B.E., D.L., T.D., who was the Chief Education Officer of the City of Leeds before his retirement, who came to know Dorothy L. Sayers and her husband quite well during the precise period we are considering. Colonel Taylor's recollections, which are of great interest in several contexts, have not previously been published. The affair of *The Nebuly Coat*, already discussed in another essay in this book, I owe entirely to his meeting with Miss Sayers.

When Colonel Taylor was at Oxford, he spent regular holidays during the Long Vacation in Kirkcudbright. His uncle was the artist, Charles Oppenheimer, who lived with his wife at 14, High Street, Kirkcudbright, and Colonel Taylor was in the habit of spending some three weeks with his uncle and aunt each autumn from 1929 to 1932. It was at this period that Miss Sayers and her husband, Captain Fleming (as he was always called in Scotland) made a practice of taking the adjoining house in High Street, No. 14A, for holidays each September, and became friendly with the Oppenheimers and their nephew. The Flemings frequently came to No. 14 for drinks, although Colonel Taylor does not recall visiting No. 14A himself. He has a very clear recollection of these meetings with Dorothy L. Sayers and her husband.

In Colonel Taylor's opinion, the description of Miss Sayers on pp. 99–100 of *Such a Strange Lady* is not a flattering one. Her hat, for example, was striking and becoming, and he is certain that it was not a 'parson's hat'. Her best feature was her beautiful speaking voice. She was very proud of having been at Somerville, and told Colonel Taylor that one day she would like to write a book about Wimsey with an Oxford background, although confessing that she was without knowledge of life in men's colleges. Her daily life in Kirkcudbright was quiet and regular, she and her husband spending most of their mornings in the town shopping and talking to friends. Her afternoons were devoted to her literary work. Colonel Taylor noticed that Fleming was fond of whisky, and frequented public-houses in the vicinity. From his conversations with Fleming, Colonel Taylor judged that he did not follow any gainful occupation at this period. He was knowledgeable about cars and drove an MG, and claimed to have driven at Brooklands in earlier years.

Colonel Taylor told me that he is certain that either Miss Sayers or Fleming said that the latter gave some help in the practical details of the incident of the car and the bicycle and the alibi of John Ferguson described in Chapters 27 and 28 of *Five Red Herrings*, published in 1931, and upon which Miss Sayers was working in 1930. Colonel Taylor is convinced that Fleming tested the journey and its timing and practicability for his wife, who prided herself upon meticulous accuracy in matters of this kind .He is equally certain, however, from his many conversations with both persons concerned, and with Fleming's obvious intellectual limitations compared with his wife's literary skill and learning, that the former's contributions to the Wimsey novels were limited to occasional practical help with isolated incidents such as the one described, in which Fleming's experience was useful. Colonel Taylor's evidence confirms, it may be thought, the conclusions of the earlier chapter in this book dealing with the claims of Mrs Ann Schruers.

Of equal importance is Colonel Taylor's belief that the couple were on good terms, but that Miss Sayers was unquestionably the dominant partner in the marriage. She was a brilliant and amusing conversationalist, entirely overshadowing her husband.

Another reason why we can be fairly sure that there was no hostility on the part of Miss Sayers towards her husband in these early years of their marriage is that her attitude towards his war experience was undoubtedly one of compassion. He had lost two brothers in the First World War, and a third had been seriously wounded. The war had been a hard one for Fleming himself, and had left mental if not physical scars. Miss Sayers' sympathetic word-picture of Captain George Fentiman in *The Unpleasantness at the Bellona Club*, published in 1928, seems to me to be of significance in this regard, as I have said.

I believe that Miss Sayers' motivation in writing *The Documents in the Case* was an entirely literary one, and that the germ of the decision to do so can be found in her Introduction to *Great Short Stories of Detection, Mystery and Horror*, published in 1928, which in my opinion was a significant year for her. She already had to her credit *Whose Body?* (1923), *Clouds of Witness* (1926), *Unnatural Death* (1927), *The Unpleasantness at the Bellona Club* (1928) and *Lord Peter Views the Body* (1928), the latter being a collection of short stories featuring Wimsey.[1] She had established herself and her aristocratic detective firmly with the reading public, as is evidenced by the fact that second editions of her books were appearing. *Whose Body?* was republished in 1925, as was *Clouds of Witness* in 1927. She had found an American market from the beginning. She could count herself a successful writer, and her Introduction to *Great Short Stories*, forty pages in length and devoted almost wholly to the history of the detective story, established her as the leading literary critic in her chosen subject at that time. I fancy that October 1928, when the Introduction was published, was the first watershed in her literary life, when she could afford to pause to consider her

---

[1] This book was published in November 1928, one month after *Great Short Stories of Detection, Mystery and Horror*. On p. 49 of their *An Annotated Guide to the Works of Dorothy L. Sayers*, however, Harman and Burger tell us that the stories 'had previously been published in several periodicals', but without further details.

position and to indulge in experiment, in the reasonable certainty that anything she now chose to write would find a ready publisher. I venture to think that the truth of this suggestion can be demonstrated by three examples.

Page 39 of the Introduction is headed 'Love Interest', and in the dissertation which follows Miss Sayers is severely critical of the fact that 'some of the finest detective-stories are marred by a conventional love-story, irrelevant to the action and perfunctorily worked in'. The books of Mr Austin Freeman are mildly castigated on these grounds, but with the saving clause that 'You can skip the love-passages if you like, and nothing is lost'. On the other hand, she is merciless in regard to 'the heroes who insist on fooling about after young women when they ought to be putting their minds to the job of detection'. In some extreme examples of behaviour of this kind by the detective which she instances, Miss Sayers takes the view that 'the whole story is impeded and its logical development ruined'. She adds that the instances in which the love-story is an integral part of the plot are extremely rare, and cites as one example her favourite *The Moonstone* by Wilkie Collins, where the entire plot relies on the love for Franklin Blake of both Rachel Verinder and Rosanna Spearman. More significant, perhaps, is her wholly admiring reference to E. C. Bentley's *Trent's Last Case* and 'the still harder problem of the detective in love', in which 'Trent's love for Mrs Manderson is an integral part of the plot'. Can we doubt that this historical and literary analysis led to Miss Sayers herself deciding to write *Strong Poison*, in which Wimsey falls in love with Harriet Vane as she faces trial for the murder of her former lover, Philip Boyes? Mr Harmon and Miss Burger say on p. 17 of their book:

> What made Miss Sayers suddenly bring love into the Wimsey stories it is not known; it may be that it just fell in as the story progressed.

I dissent from this speculation for reasons I have made plain. The probability that the introduction of Harriet Vane and a love interest as essential ingredients of *Strong Poison* in 1930 was an experiment by Miss Sayers to see whether, like E. C. Bentley, she too could overcome 'the still harder problem of the detective in love' would seem to be increased by the fact that her next Wimsey story, *Five Red Herrings*, published in 1931, contains no mention of Harriet Vane.

In an article 'Why I killed Peter Wimsey' published in the *Sunday Despatch* of 22 December 1957, Val Gielgud described an interview with Miss Sayers in her Witham home shortly before her death. He reported her as saying:

> I wrote detective stories because when I came down from the university, I had to earn my living. And I preferred writing to other ways of making bread and butter that I tried. But that does not mean that the writing of detective stories was the sort of writing which I preferred. It was certainly not the sort of occupation for which I had been trained. . . . What I want to emphasise is that as long ago as 1930 [*sic*] I published a translation of the French 12th-century romance *Tristan in Brittany*. But you could hardly expect me to earn my living by writing that kind of thing.

On page 11 of her Introduction to *Great Short Stories of Detection, Mystery and Horror* Miss Sayers was discussing the occurrence of the principles of detection in the literature of ancient times from which, indeed, the first four stories in the book are taken. She mentions the story of Tristan, and how the king's spy spread flour on the floor between Tristan's bed and that of Iseult, a scheme which Tristan defeated by leaping from one bed to the other. This ancient romance was therefore in her mind in 1928, contained as it was in the research material she had gathered for the historical *Introduction*. One wonders if she thought it possible that her reputation and popularity as a writer was now sufficiently established for her to risk the experiment of publishing with success the kind of work she considered her standard of scholarship deserved. I think that she did, and the result was that in July, 1929 Ernest Benn published *Tristan in Brittany. Being the fragments of The Romance of Tristan, written in the XII century, by Thomas the Anglo-Norman. Drawn from the French into the English by Dorothy Leigh Sayers, M.A., sometime scholar of Somerville College, Oxford. With an Introduction by George Saintsbury*. It was a book of 220 pages in brown cloth. My copy, which is in mint condition, was presented to me as a gift by the late Frank Beckwith, the former Librarian of the

Leeds Library. It is not hard to find even today, despite the fact that I can trace no subsequent edition in *The English Catalogue*. The only other books by Miss Sayers listed in *The English Catalogue* in 1929 were cheap new editions of *Whose Body?*, *Clouds of Witness* and *Lord Peter Views the Body*. If the transla-lation of *Tristan* was an experiment in published scholarship, therefore, with its origins in the Introduction to *Great Short Stories*, it must be reckoned as financially premature. She returned to the writing of detective stories with the publication of *The Documents in the Case* and *Strong Poison* respectively in July and October 1930, a course she was to continue for another nine years.

The third experiment by Miss Sayers at this crucial period in her career as a writer was *The Documents in the Case*. As I have tried to show in the early pages of this essay it was undoubtedly inspired by her keen admiration for *The Moonstone* and *Trent's Last Case*, with their ingenious and effective literary mechan-isms, Collins' epistolary presentation by means of individual narratives, and the shift of viewpoint employed by Bentley. From her point of view, the introduction of Wimsey or any other detective would not have been possible within the framework of *The Documents in the Case*, in which the narratives and impres-sions of all the characters are placed at the disposal of the reader. In a footnote on page 36 of the all-important Introduction to *Great Short Stories of Detection, Mystery and Horror* she laid down the rule that no episode must be made known to the reader which does not come within the cognisance of the inves-tigator:

> Thus, the reader's interest in *The Deductions of Colonel Gore* (Lynn Brock) is sensibly diminished by his knowing (as Gore does not) that it was Cecil Arndale who witnessed the scene between Mrs Melhuish and Barrington at the beginning of the book.

In *The Documents in the Case* the identity of the possible murderer is never in doubt. The mystery lies in the question as to whether George Harrison was murdered, or whether he, an expert on edible fungi, had poisoned himself by accident. Within this plot framework the epistolary presentation is perfect for the purpose. *The Documents in the Case* was also an experiment in collaboration, which Miss Sayers had not attempted before. It was a necessary experiment, for it followed that since the mystery to be solved was whether Harrison was poisoned by accident or design, the secret must inevitably be medical or scientific. As Miss Sayers was not a scientific person, she would clearly need technical assistance in the writing of such a book. Precisely as in the other matters discussed in the earlier paragraphs of this essay, I am convinced that the clue we seek as to her thoughts and actions at this time lies in the pages of her Introduction to *Great Short Stories &c.*, written in what I have come to regard as her first literary climacteric of 1928. On page 31, in that part of her dissertation headed 'The Scientific Detective', she wrote of the boom in detective stories in the 'nineties and thereafter, which began under the aegis of Sherlock Holmes. She said that the long series which appeared from the pens of Mrs L. T. Meade (afterwards Mrs Toulmin Smith) and her two scientific collaborators around the turn of the century was of particular interest. Elizabeth Thomasina Meade (1854–1914), who during her earlier literary career had written a large number of stories for girls, turned her attention to the fruitful vein of the detective novel and short story, with the necessary aid of two co-authors. Both wrote under pseudonyms, 'Clifford Halifax' and 'Robert Eustace', and the first of these collections, *Stories from the Diary of a Doctor* was written with 'Clifford Halifax' and was published in 1893.

Miss Sayers did not reveal the identity of either of Mrs Meade's pseudonymous co-authors in her account of the matter, but she did say that the last of the long series of these joint works was *The Sorceress of the Strand*, written in collaboration with Robert Eustace and published in 1902. The first two collections of mystery stories written by Mrs Meade with Robert Eustace were both published in 1898. *The Brotherhood of the Seven Kings* was serialised in *The Strand*, commencing in January 1898, and *A Master of Mysteries* was published as a book in the same year. It is clear that in 1928 Miss Sayers respected the work of Robert Eustace, for she included in *Great Short Stories of Detection, Mystery and Horror* two stories of which he was part author. They were 'The Face in the Dark' by L. T. Meade and Robert Eustace, published in *The London*

Magazine in 1903, and 'The Tea-Leaf' by Edgar Jepson and Robert Eustace, published in *The Strand Magazine* of 1925.

There has never been any doubt about the identity of 'Clifford Halifax', despite the fact that Miss Sayers was careful to conceal the real names of both Mrs Meade's co-authors in her short history of the collaborations in 1928. He was Dr Edgar Beaumont, and was a distinguished physician of wide experience. He held the degrees of M.D.(Durham), M.R.C.S., L.R.C.P. (London), and was a Prizeman in Anatomy and Physiology. He was the author of an important paper, 'Successful Extirpation of Spleen for Traumatic Rupture', published in *The Lancet* in 1902. He was a partner in a successful medical practice in Norwood, London, and was a Divisional Surgeon of the Metropolitan Police. We may think that Mrs L. T. Meade had no need to look further for a collaborator who was an expert on medical science. The books they wrote together, which included *Stories from the Diary of a Doctor*, already mentioned, *Dr Rumsey's Patient*, 1896 and *The Diary of a Doctor*, 1910, had a genuine scientific background. They were of a different calibre, although not perhaps so successful with the reading public, as the string of exciting thrillers Mrs Meade wrote with Robert Eustace, as I hope to show. The death of Dr Beaumont was reported in *The Medical Directory* of 1922, however, so that his collaboration in *The Documents in the Case*, had Miss Sayers wished it was not possible.

The Documents in the Case was a very successful book, and was republished many times. It is still in print today. I think it likely, however, that Miss Sayers did not obtain any permanent satisfaction from it, for a reason which I mentioned in passing in the early pages of this essay. I said that it lacked scientific accuracy. Miss Sayers knew that it did shortly after its publication and admitted it both in a radio talk and in print. In an article, 'Trials and Sorrows of a Mystery Writer', published in *The Listener* of 6 January 1932 (being the text of a broadcast talk delivered by her on 29 December 1931) Miss Sayers referred to *The Documents in the Case* as a book she wrote with Robert Eustace, in which 'a gigantic howler was made', as a result of the joint authors relying upon unsound outside advice.

As has been said earlier, Howard Lathom murdered his

mistress's husband, George Harrison, by introducing synthetic muscarine secretly into a dish of harmless edible fungi, thus giving the impression that some poisonous fungi containing natural organic muscarine had been gathered and eaten by mistake. The presence of synthetic muscarine and the fact of murder was discovered by means of the polariscope. Miss Sayers wrote in January 1932:

> The poisons would give the same chemical analysis, and the only way to distinguish them would be by examining them through the polariscope, when one would find that the natural poison twisted the ray of light, while the synthetic didn't. We consulted experts, who told us that this idea was perfectly sound, and so we set to work. . . . Well, it wasn't long before we got the inevitable letter, from a very polite professor of chemistry, convicting us of a gigantic howler. Our general theory was quite all right, but muscarine was an exception. Natural muscarine didn't play fair. It didn't twist the ray of polarised light any more than the synthetic kind. If we had picked, for instance, on conium, which is a poison you get from hemlock, that would have worked perfectly. There was nothing wrong with the plot except those infernal toadstools. And the moral of that is, that it is always very dangerous to meddle with poisonous toad-stools.

This mistake must have seemed a great nuisance to Miss Sayers, who prided herself on the accuracy of the details of her books, as was natural to a scholar of her standard. She was not a scientific person, and the only blame she could take to herself in the matter, we may think, was her reliance upon Robert Eustace in his choice of the experts who were consulted. That she was annoyed about the mistake would seem to be demonstrated by her treatment of Robert Eustace in the matter of *Have His Carcase*, which was published in 1932, about which I shall have something to say in the next chapter. Oddly enough, the article in *The Listener* seems to have attracted little attention, and neither the authors or the publishers of the later editions of *The Documents in the Case* seem to have considered it necessary to make any correction.

One curious incident followed the publication of Miss Sayers' article in *The Listener* of 6 January 1932. About seventeen miles from Miss Sayers' home in Witham at that time is the village of

Hockley, also in Essex. Seven days after the article appeared a gentleman living in Spa Road, Hockley made and signed his last will, leaving everything he possessed to his wife. The date of 'thirteenth day of January 1932' is embodied in the first three lines of the short will, comprising a single sheet of foolscap. The will thus hastily made was witnessed by Mrs Alice Louisa Griffin, also of Spa Road, Hockley and Roland Johnson, the sub-postmaster of Hockley. Five days later on 18 January 1932, the testator died of 'influenza and myocardial degeneration'. He was described on his death entry as being 76 years old, and a 'retired author'. He used the pseudonym of 'Robert Eustace'.

VII

DOROTHY L. SAYERS AND
ROBERT EUSTACE

WITH some of the facts and motivations concerning the writing of *The Documents in the Case* now established, I revert to Mrs Hitchman's published views on the book, despite my disagreement with her general theme, because a paragraph on page 75 of her *Such a Strange Lady* will introduce to the reader (as it did to me over three years ago) one of the most fascinating literary puzzles it has been my good fortune to encounter:

> The outcome of whatever troubled her was *The Documents in the Case*, the most revealing of her detective books. It is the only one which does not feature Lord Peter Wimsey, although one character from the Wimsey books, Sir James Lubbock, the Home Office analyst, does appear. It is also the only one in which she acknowledges collaboration. *Busman's Honeymoon*, in which she was joined by Miss Muriel St. Clair [*sic*] Byrne, was originally a play. The only sign of Robert Eustace's hand in *The Documents in the Case* is the medical information, though why she needed to acknowledge medical assistance for this book, and not for *Have His Carcase* is not clear. 'Robert Eustace' was the pen-name of Dr Eustace Robert Barton, M.R.C.S., L.R.C.P., who helped several writers, including Mrs L. T. Meade and Edgar Jepson, with medical details, particularly about poison. Sir Hugh Greene, to whom I am indebted for this information, has traced Dr Barton's activities from the 1890s to 1947, after which he seems to have completely disappeared. Nowhere is his death recorded. Rather appropriate for one who lived so mysteriously.

A preliminary comment that must be made on Mrs Hitchman's exposition is that Miss Sayers did not 'acknowledge medical assistance' from Robert Eustace in *The Documents in the Case*. Their names appeared on the title-page as joint authors, and that is all. There is no indication in the book of the extent of their respective contributions. I think that it is right for Mrs Hitchman to say that it is odd that Miss Sayers did not acknowledge the medical help that was clearly needed for the writing of *Have His Carcase*, but wrong for her to assert that *The Documents in the Case* is the only novel in which she conceded that she received advice. On the verso of the title-page of *Have His Carcase*, indeed, Miss Sayers gratefully thanked 'Mr John Rhode, who gave me generous help with all the hard bits'.

Have His Carcase opens with the grisly discovery by Harriet Vane of the body of a gigolo, Paul Alexis, his throat literally 'cut from ear to ear', on a rock by the sea-shore. The plot revolves in part around the timing of the murder being hopelessly confused by the fact, unknown to the investigators, that Alexis was a 'bleeder'. Miss Sayers could not have written the book without a reasonable knowledge of haemophilia. She did not rely for this information upon John Rhode, but upon Robert Eustace, who, as the reader will learn, went to considerable trouble to ascertain from a specialist in the disease at Edinburgh University all the facts Miss Sayers needed to know on the subject. Why this generous help was deliberately not acknowledged is a mystery. Miss Sayers may well have been annoyed at having publicly to admit the 'gigantic howler' over the properties of muscarine in *The Documents in the Case*, for which her collaborator had evidently obtained the unreliable particulars from a 'young friend' at Oxford. On the other hand, the information in regard to haemophilia which Robert Eustace supplied to her from his 'kind and eminent young friend' at Edinburgh was detailed and accurate. To ignore this assistance totally in *Have His Carcase*, and yet to thank John Rhode as she did, seems most unfair on the face of it. Whether she had some other reason for suddenly wishing to dissociate her name from that of Robert Eustace at this time will be examined in this essay. On the surface, the incident is not to Miss Sayers' credit, which is one of the reasons why later in these pages I have discussed the positive evidence

demonstrating that the attitude of Robert Eustace's distinguished father towards his son was one of contemptuous dislike.

Who was Robert Eustace? I must say now that the name of
the 'retired author' who had unquestionably used the pseudonym
'Robert Eustace', and who died at Hockley in Essex twelve days
after Miss Sayers had revealed in print that the plot of *The
Documents in the Case* was based on 'a gigantic howler', was
Eustace Fraser Rawlins. I am frank to say that for some time I
thought my discovery of his death entry and the curious coincidence of the surrounding cirumstances settled the matter, when
looked at in combination with the standard sources of information which I naturally consulted. Further investigation
proved, however, that the solution was not so simple as it
seemed.

The identity of 'Robert Eustace' presents an intricate
problem for the bibliographer, and I have enjoyed a long and
stimulating correspondence with Sir Hugh Greene on the
subject. So far as I am aware my solution of it (which is not a
simple one but with which Sir Hugh agrees) has not previously
been suggested by any literary commentator. Mrs Hitchman's
identification of 'Robert Eustace' with Dr Eustace Robert
Barton is not confirmed by other writers on the history of
detective fiction. Thus Ordean A. Hagen, in his massive
Who Done it? A Guide to Detective, Mystery and Suspense Fiction
(London & New York 1969), tells us on p. 136 that Robert
Eustace was the pen-name used by Eustace Rawlins, who
collaborated with L. T. Meade (p. 315) and Dorothy L.
Sayers (p. 366). These statements are confirmed by Eric
Quayle, who on p. 93 of his *The Collector's Book of Detective
Fiction* (London, 1972) remarks:

> L. T. Meade compensated for her lack of scientific and medical
> knowledge by using the services of at least two male collaborators
> who were skilled in both these fields. They were 'Clifford Halifax'
> (Dr Edgar Beaumont) and 'Robert Eustace' (E. Rawlins), who
> later wrote *The Hidden Treasures of Egypt* [1925] under the same
> pseudonym.

When writing of the work of Dorothy L. Sayers on page 101 of
the same book Mr Quayle tells us:

In *The Documents in the Case,* Benn (1930), she relied for her scientific knowledge on her collaborator 'Robert Eustace', who, it will be remembered, had assisted L. T. Meade in a similar manner some 32 years earlier. This novel has been described as a technical masterpiece.

In parenthesis, I may say that it would seem from Mr Quayle's last sentence that he was unaware that forty years before his book was published Miss Sayers had conceded in print and on the radio 'the gigantic howler' over the properties of muscarine. I mention the point merely to confirm my own belief, expressed earlier in this book, that the admission of the mistake does not appear to have become widely known.

The statements of both Mr Hagen and Mr Quayle are confirmed by the *British Museum General Catalogue of Printed Books,* which has no entry for Dr Eustace Robert Barton. In col. 239 of vol. 199, however, we find the single entry, 'Rawlins, (E), *See* Eustace (Robert), *pseud.'* If we turn to the list of works by Dorothy L. Sayers in vol. 213, we find in col. 1015 that the joint authors of *The Documents in the Case* are there recorded as 'Sayers (D.L.) and Eustace (Robert) *pseud.* (i.e. E. Rawlins)'. When we turn finally to the entry for 'Eustace (Robert) *pseud.* (i.e. E. Rawlins)', we find it at the head of over half a dozen entries of books in which he is stated to have collaborated, starting in the 1890s with L. T. Meade, followed by the joint authorship with Gertrude Warden of *The Stolen Pearl* in 1903 and with Dorothy L. Sayers in *The Documents in the Case* in 1930, this being the last in order of date. The penultimate item, with a date of 1925, was a novel written by the author alone. It was *The Hidden Treasures of Egypt. A Romance,* published by Simpkin, Marshall & Co. Before this entry came another novel written by Robert Eustace without collaboration, *A Human Bacillus. The Story of a Strange Character,* published in 1907 by John Long.

Another source to which the bibliographer naturally turns in investigations of this kind is Halkett and Laing's *Dictionary of Anonymous and Pseudonymous Literature* (7 volumes, London and Edinburgh, 1926–34 with two supplementary volumes published in 1956 and 1972). Here we find on p. 6 of vol. iii and on p. 418 of vol. vi that the real name of 'Robert Eustace' is stated to be E. Rawlins.

The great American work of bibliographical reference, the counterpart of the *British Museum General Catalogue*, is the *National Union Catalog* based on the Library of Congress at Washington, D.C., which has replaced the old *Library of Congress Catalog*. It was of additional interest to find the entry in vol. 482 for *The Hidden Treasures of Egypt. A Romance. . . .* by Robert Eustace (*pseud.*) catalogued under the name of the author, 'Rawlins, Eustace, 1854—', which gives the added information of the author's year of birth, and enables us to calculate that he would be in his seventies when *The Documents in the Case* was published in 1930. On p. 448 of vol. 163 this is confirmed by a general entry with no book title reading simply, 'Eustace R., *pseud. see* Rawlins, Eustace, 1854—'. Another very interesting entry in the *National Union Catalog* takes us back to the turn of the century and *A Master of Mysteries*, first published by Ward, Lock & Co. in 1898. This book consisted of six mystery stories told in the first person by a psychical investigator named Bell, who remarked of himself, that 'from my earliest youth the weird and mysterious had an irresistible fascination for me'. The second of these stories was 'The Warder of the Door', and concerned a curse which had rested on a family named Clinton since 1400.

> And in this cell its coffin lieth, the coffin which hath not human shape, for which reason no holy ground receiveth it. Here it shall rest to curse ye family of ye Clintons from generation to generation. And for this reason, as soon as the soul shall pass from the body of each first-born, which is the heir, it shall become the warder of the door by day and by night. Day and night shall his spirit stand by the door, to keep the door closed till the son shall release the spirit of the father from the watch and take his place, till his son in turn shall die. And who so entereth into the cell shall be the prisoner of the soul that guardeth the door till it shall let him go.

Over thirty years later this blood-curdling tale was reprinted in *The Great Weird Stories*, edited by A. Neale and published in New York in 1929. On page 672 of volume 550 of *The National Union Catalog*, credit for the inclusion of 'The Warder of the Door' in *The Great Weird Stories* is given to 'Smith, Elizabeth Thomasina (Meade) and Rawlins, Eustace, 1854—'. The fact that the flavour of the stories comprising *A Master of Mysteries* does not suggest that much medical or scientific knowledge was used to write them is further exemplified in the fifth, 'How Siva Spoke', of which the following is an extract from the dialogue:

> While he had been speaking to me he had been gazing at the idol; now he walked a few steps away and turned his back on it. 'Sooner or later I must obey him;' he said in a feeble voice 'but the thing is driving me crazed—crazed.'
>
> 'What is it?' I asked: 'tell me, I beseech you.'
>
> 'I cannot, it is too awful—it relates to the one I love best in all the world. The sacrifice is too horrible, and yet I am drawn to it—I am drawn to the performing of an awful deed by a terrific power. Ask me no more, Mr Bell; I see by your face that I have your pity.'
>
> 'You have, truly', I answered.

In the same year as the publication of *A Master of Mysteries*, L. T. Meade and Robert Eustace also collaborated in *The Brotherhood of the Seven Kings*. It first appeared as a serial in *The Strand Magazine*, commencing in the issue of January 1898 and continuing in ten monthly episodes throughout the half-yearly volumes XV and XVI. It was published as a book by Ward, Lock & Co. in 1899. It was a series of adventures in which the hero, Norman Head, assisted by a lawyer friend, Colin Dufrayer, outwitted the machinations of a Mafia-like secret society led by the infamous but physically fascinating Mme Koluchy, a woman who 'dazzled by her beauty and intellect'. The authors were fortunate in having Sidney Paget as their illustrator. The initials 'SP' familiar to all Sherlock Holmes enthusiasts are discernible on all the plates except the full-page frontispiece to volume XVI of *The Strand Magazine*, illustrating 'The Iron Circlet', the seventh story of *The Brotherhood of the Seven Kings*. (See illustration opposite p. 18).

Neither scientific nor medical expertise are suggested by the illustration or the text of 'The Iron Circlet'. The scene is a sea-cave at night, in which a small raft is floating on the ebbing tide. The hero, bound hand and foot, is securely lashed in a standing position to the raft, awaiting slow decapitation from a circular metal device around his neck and suspended by a chain from the roof of the cave, as the raft slowly sinks on the receding tide.

My neck was fixed to the chain above, my feet to the timber in the sea below. The words of my terrible sentence burst upon me now with all their fiendish meaning. As the tide went down the whole weight of the raft would gradually drag my body from my head. The horror of such a fearful doom almost benumbed my faculties, and I stood as one already dead, being swayed by the light swell that found its way into the cave.

Examples of other titles of similar calibre in *The Brotherhood of the Seven Kings* are 'The Doom', 'At the Edge of the Crater', 'The Winged Assassin' and 'The Star-Shaped Marks'.

The prolific and indefatigable L. T. Meade and Robert Eustace contributed *Stories of the Sanctuary Club* in five episodes to volume XVIII of *The Strand Magazine* commencing in July 1899. The same title was published as a book by Ward, Lock & Co. in 1900. The first story, 'The Death Chair', is perhaps a sufficient indication of the degree (or lack) of scientific knowledge contained in these adventurous yarns. The body of the murdered man, John Ingram, was found among the gorse bushes of Wimbledon Common about three hundred yards from Roe House, the residence of a sinister Spaniard, Don Santos, who had good reason to wish Ingram dead. Roe House is shielded from the common by a thick belt of tall trees.

The problem facing the investigators, Paul Cato and his friend Chetwynd, is twofold. Almost every bone in the luckless Ingram's body is broken, and the soft ground around the body shows not the slightest trace of any other person being involved. The preliminary view is that the only conceivable solution of the mystery is that Ingram must have fallen from a balloon. The secret was exposed by Cato at the risk of his life, after dining with Don Santos at Roe House, where his host attempted to murder him by the same method he had used to kill Ingram. Invited to conclude the evening on the veranda, it being 'a beautiful starlit night and perfectly warm', he was urged by Don Santos to sit in a particular deck-chair. His life was saved by his friend Chetwynd, who had discovered the deadly secret of Roe House.

He rushed towards me, his eyes alight with terror, his voice hoarse with fear. 'For God's sake, Paul, get out of that chair,' he cried; 'jump for your life!' There was not time to be even surprised. I made one bound from the chair, and at the same instant something whirled through the air close behind me. There was a dull clang. Chetwynd, gripping my arm, pointed up. Neither of us could speak. Fixed at the extremity of a huge steel spring which had been disguised as one of the planks of the veranda, the chair had flown up in a great arc above us, the spring had dashed against the bars of the iron railing, and the chair thus checked suddenly in its flight was still quivering to and fro from the terrific shock of the impact!

Chetwynd showed Cato a small secret room under the veranda, containing a cogged wheel and ratchet, which could be wound by a handle. A long steel chain was used to wind down the huge steel spring until it was level with the veranda floor, complete with the attached deck-chair. A cord drew back the catch which released the spring. 'Well, you saw the result for yourself. One moment more and it would have flung you over the tree-tops and out on to the common, three hundred yards away. Your dead body would have been found there in the morning. Just as in Ingram's case, there would have been no clue.'

I invited the opinion of my stepson, Leslie McMorris of Christ's College, Cambridge, a distinguished mechanical scientist of wide experience, on the feasability of 'The Death Chair'. He was kind enough to contribute his view, as I asked him to do, in terms comprehensible to a layman like myself:

The concept of human projectiles being launched across the tree-tops of Wimbledon Common by Don Santos' satanical device stretches one's credulity if not one's imagination. Images of steam catapult aircraft launchers, fighter pilot ejector seats and human cannon ball acts at the circus cross the mind. However, the Spaniard's equipment was limited to the mechanisms of the last century contained in a small room, which makes nonsense of the idea. The victim would require a veranda escape velocity of some 250 m.p.h. in order to clear (closely) the trees, and be trajected into the gorse bushes at 300 yards range. A force in excess of 20 tons would be required to give the adequate momentary acceleration, whilst the chair must have been fabricated from some incredibly strong material. The force briefly imparted to the seat of the projecting incumbent would be equivalent in a static circus analogy to four large African elephants simultaneously sitting with their full combined weight on the comfortable deck chair.

There is no entry for Eustace Rawlins in *The Medical Directory*, which means that he was not a medical man. He had no entry in *Who's Who*, nor does his name appear in the lists of members of British universities that were available when he was a young man. The *Catalogue of Copyright Entries*, pt. 1, n.s.v. 23, p. 900 shows that *The Hiddden Treasures of Egypt. A Romance*, published by Simpkin, Marshall, Hamilton, Kent & Co. Ltd. in 1925, was written by Eustace Rawlins under the pseudonym of Robert Eustace. In 1925 Mr Rawlins was living at 'Croylands', Eversley Crescent, Isleworth, Middlesex, which was a good address.

The bibliographical references to Rawlins' year of birth were checked at the General Register Office. His birth appeared in the index as having taken place in the Andover district in the July–September quarter of 1854. If he was indeed Dorothy L. Sayers' collaborator in *The Documents in the Case*, as is recorded in the *British Museum Catalogue* and elsewhere, then it was reasonable to suppose that his death occurred in 1930 at the earliest. The indexes at the General Register Office were searched forwards from that year, and his death entry on 18 January 1932 at Hockley in Essex was located, as was described at the end of the preceding chapter. His stated age of 76, presumably supplied by his widow, was understated by one year, this kind of mistake being common enough in my experience. It was useful to obtain from the same document his full name, and the information that he had been an author.

In 1942, in his *Murder for Pleasure. The Life and Times of the Detective Story*, Howard Haycraft wrote on pp. 136–7 that Miss Sayers' *The Documents in the Case* was 'written with "Robert Eustace", the pseudonymous scientific collaborator of a long line of authors'. Two years later, James Sandoe, in his 'Contribution toward a Bibliography of Dorothy L. Sayers' in the *Bulletin of Bibliography* (May–August, 1944) said the same thing. In 1946, however, *The Art of the Mystery Story, A Collection of Critical Essays. Edited and with a Commentary by Howard Haycraft* was published in New York. James Sandoe was a contributor, and in his 'Reader's Guide to Crime' it was stated that the real name of 'Robert Eustace' was Eustace Robert Barton. The comparison between lack of knowledge in

1944 and this definite identification in 1946 suggested that some new information had been published between these two dates, a conjecture that proved to be well-founded.

In 1945 the 1938–1942 volume of the *Cumulative Book Index. A World List of Books in the English Language* was published by the H. W. Wilson Co. of Bronx, New York. On p. 182 Robert Eustace was stated to be the pseudonym of Eustace Robert Barton, an entry slightly confused by the contradiction on p. 2134 (presumably a misprint) that the pseudonymous collaborator 'Robert Eustace' with Dorothy L. Sayers in *The Documents in the Case* was 'R. E. Barton'. A letter was written to the publishers of the *Cumulative Book Index* on 21 August 1978, asking if it would be possible for the evidence for this attribution to be quoted. The H. W. Wilson Co. responded with a courteous and apologetic reply, of which the relevant extract reads:

> The entry, Eustace Robert Barton, found in our 1938–1942 volume of *Cumulative Book Index* was obtained from the December, 1943 issue of the *Wilson Library Bulletin*. Unfortunately the *Bulletin* no longer has the records to support this attribution. We are sorry that we could not find the original source of our information.

With this letter was enclosed a copy of p. 294 of the December 1943 issue of the *Wilson Library Bulletin*, which consisted of two columns of death reports, one of which reads:

> October 14. Eustace Robert Barton (Robert Eustace) writer and collaborator with Dorothy L. Sayers; at Newport, England; 75.

The date of death was two days late, but the year, age and place were correct. This meant that despite Mrs Hitchman's assertion that the death was never traced, it was in fact published in America within three months of its occurrence, coupled with the information (the evidence for which could not be confirmed) that he was the co-author of *The Documents in the Case*. His death entry was obtained without difficulty, for I assumed that the American description of Newport, England was more likely to mean Newport in Wales than the Essex village of that name. Eustace Robert Barton, aged 75, of 204 Stow Hill, Newport, Mon., described as 'an assistant medical officer in a mental hospital', died on 12 October 1943 at the Royal Gwent Hospital at Newport. The cause of death was certified as

'Cardiac failure. Haematemesis'. The unusual entry in the column 'Signature, description and residence of informant' was 'John H. Bass. Causing the body to be buried. Penybont, College Crescent, Caerlon, Mon.'

Dr Barton left a total estate of £128 10s. 11d. His will was made and signed twenty years before his death, on 30 November 1923. He described himself simply as a physician, and nowhere in his will was there any indication that he was or had been a writer, either by mention of disposition of future royalties, copyrights or in any other way. In his will he gave his address as St. Gwithians, Carbis Bay, Cornwall. It was witnessed by Caroline Frances Turner, spinster, and Margaret Anne Sellon, widow, both of whom gave their permanent address as St. Gwithians. Dr Barton left the whole of his estate, such as it was, to Hugh Gilbert Rene Sellon, presumably the son of the widowed Mrs Sellon. As we shall see, investigation has shown that Dr Barton lived for a part of each year at St. Gwithians for many years. It seems, in those distant days at least, to have been a private hotel catering for semi-permanent guests, and it is a reasonable assumption that Dr Barton and Mrs Sellon's son had become close friends. It also seems fair to presume from the will that in 1923 Dr Barton, in his mid-fifties, was either a widower or, much more probably in view of the results of my studies of his life, had never married. A further deduction, supported by evidence subsequently to be discussed, is the likelihood that Dr Barton was on bad terms with his sister and two brothers.

He clearly had a fear of being buried alive. One of the provisions of his short will was that 'before any preliminary steps are taken for my burial my Executors shall obtain from a duly qualified medical practitioner a certificate in writing that life is extinct and to be certain on this point he shall have divided completely the Aorta for which operation he shall receive the sum of Ten Guineas'.

At this stage in the investigation my inclination was to believe the evidence of the *British Museum Catalogue* and the other sources of information I have quoted, which all pointed to Eustace Fraser Rawlins being the real name of 'Robert Eustace'. This inclination was inferentially strengthened by a letter from my friend Leonard N. Beck, the Curator of Special Collections in the Library of Congress, with whom I have corresponded for many years in regard to bibliographical problems. In his letter of 14 September 1978, Leonard Beck told me that 'in the leisurely 1920s the Library's cataloguers were encouraged to correspond directly with the author or publisher of a book that presented problems', a remark which strengthened my faith in the 'Rawlins' entries in the *National Union Catalog*. On the other hand, the will of Eustace Fraser Rawlins puzzled me, despite the fact that unlike that of Eustace Robert Barton, it did have something to say about his literary work.

He left everything of which he died possessed to his 'dear devoted wife Emily Rawlins absolutely'. These assets included specific sums of money bequeathed to him by his sister and grandfather (described in the will as £800 and £1,000 respectively) together with 'all my goods, copyrights and everything of which I am now possessed'. Among the copyrights named in the will was that of *The Hidden Treasures of Egypt*, which had run into three editions and had been made into a film, 'fully copyrighted in America as well as in all Cinema Palaces of any description copyrighted under the International Convention.'

It was evident that Rawlins was very proud of *The Hidden Treasures of Egypt*, in view of his reference to its success in his will. It was reviewed in the *Times Literary Supplement* of 4 February 1926. It was described as

> An historical novel ... presenting first the pillaging of the Egyptian tombs in the reign of Pharaoh Menenptah II by the Israelites, and especially an unscrupulous Hebrew usurer whose daughter Rachel becomes the heroine of the novel; and the whole story, as recorded in the Scriptures, of the Exodus. . . . Mr Eustace has devoted much space and care to his description of tombs, temples and ceremonies—much of the book being in the form of a narrative supposed to be adapted from the records of a high Egyptian official. There is a full and vivid description of the catastrophe of the Red Sea. Though Mr Eustace's narrative manner is sometimes humdrum (and his English not impeccable) those who like this kind of historical story will certainly read it with pleasure.

I read the remainder of the will of Eustace Fraser Rawlins with increasing perplexity, despite the uncompromising evidence of the standard works of reference and the fact that *The*

Hidden Treasures of Egypt was unquestionably published over the name of Robert Eustace as the author. He listed the copyrights of other works by him, including *Picturesque New Zealand*, for which the engravings were 'copied from my own drawings made on the spot, of which there is now no truer existing record'. Rawlins mentioned among his copyrights a drama entitled *Rinzi*, and a series of *Bijou Souvenirs* of Hampton Court, Putney and Blackheath. It will be evident from my account of the entries in the *British Museum Catalogue* that I have been unable to trace any of these publications under the names of either Eustace Rawlins or Robert Eustace, from which we must conclude that they were published either anonymously or under yet another name. Of greater importance was the fact that nowhere in the will was there any mention of the royalties from the collaboration with Dorothy L. Sayers in *The Documents in the Case* in 1930, only two years before Rawlins' death. The absence of any mention of collaboration with Mrs L. T. Meade in the series of sensational detective stories written around the turn of the century I regarded as less evidential, since it may be thought that the royalties from those publications would have petered out many years ago.

For the first time I began to wonder seriously whether there were two Robert Eustaces, a theory which has never previously been suggested by any literary commentator, using the same pseudonym and over-lapping in time. An extreme example of such over-lapping was the publication of *The Hidden Treasures of Egypt*, which *The English Catalogue* tells us appeared on the bookstalls in November 1925, only one month after the issue of *The Strand Magazine* for October of the same year, containing a detective story 'The Tea-Leaf', by Edgar Jepson and Robert Eustace, describing an apparent murder (actually a suicide designed to look like murder) in a Turkish bath, by means of a dagger made of frozen and compressed carbon dioxide concealed in a Thermos flask. I was aware that such a hypothesis would mean that both the *British Museum Catalogue* and the *National Union Catalog* contained many erroneous entries, and that distinguished modern writers on detective fiction had simply perpetuated these mistakes. Was the second Robert Eustace Dr Eustace Robert Barton, whose name appears nowhere in the *British Museum Catalogue* and whose death, according to Mrs Hitchman, had never been traced?

After some thought, I wrote to Miss Livia Gollancz, to whom I had been introduced by my friend Wilfrid Scott-Giles, O.B.E., F.S.A., the author of *The Wimsey Family*. Miss Gollancz said that her firm now had no file on Robert Eustace, but kindly suggested that I should write to Mr Peter Grose of Curtis Brown Limited, the literary agents. Mr Grose replied to my letter promptly to say that there was a collaboration agreement signed on 21 January 1929 between Miss Dorothy L. Sayers and Dr Eustace Robert Barton (writing under the name of Robert Eustace) of St. Andrew's Hospital, Northampton, to write a novel to be published by Ernest Benn Limited 'under such title as the parties may decide'. Messrs. Curtis Brown carefully checked their records, but could find no trace of their having acted for Eustace Robert Barton, either under his own name or that of Robert Eustace, on any other occasion. There can be no doubt that *The Documents in the Case* was the product of this agreement. I am also indebted to James Brabazon, who is writing a biography of Miss Sayers and with whom I have exchanged information to our mutual advantage, for letting me see two letters from Dr Barton to Miss Sayers containing the information in regard to muscarine and haemophilia culled from friends in Oxford and Edinburgh to which reference has been made earlier in this essay. In the second of these letters Dr Barton said that he had been in Cornwall for several months (he wrote from St. Gwithians, Carbis Bay) and that during 'long leisure hours' he had read and re-read *The Documents in the Case*. 'Your work in it is tremendously good', he wrote, 'and I am quite sure that it will long survive the usual flood that engulfs ephemeral fiction. My regret remains for the blunder about the optical activity, and I am glad to have the true scientific explanation as to how such should have occurred to anyone not in touch with the complexities of the matter'.[1]

[1] The explanation for the mistake over muscarine and the polariscope was quoted by Dr Barton in his letter. I think that it should be recorded for the scientifically-minded reader, but reduced to a footnote for the benefit of the faint-hearted. 'Muscarine is not in itself a protein. It is an alkaloid, though it is a breakdown product of Protein. The Proteins are most highly complex substances, none of which, as yet, have been synthesised. They all consist of complex Amino-Acids

The same letter contained the proof that Dr Barton had helped Miss Sayers with the information she needed about haemophilia to write *Have His Carcase*, for which he received no acknowledgement in that book.[1] It was at this stage in the inquiry that Sir Hugh Greene conceded in our long and interesting correspondence, in which I had told him of the discoveries I had made, that I had established what he christened the 'two fixed points' on which the ultimate solution could firmly rest. There was now no doubt whatever that the *British Museum Catalogue* and the *National Union Catalog* were incorrect in uniformly identifying 'Robert Eustace' as 'Eustace Rawlins' in all the entries under the former name. There was also now no doubt whatever that two writers had used the pseudonym 'Robert Eustace', since I had proved that Eustace Fraser Rawlins had written *The Hidden Treasures of Egypt* and that Dr Eustace Robert Barton had been the co-author of *The Documents in the Case*. It was Sir Hugh who suggested that I would be completing an important contribution to the history of detective fiction if I could offer a solution to the remaining mystery. Which of the two Robert Eustaces had collaborated with Mrs L. T. Meade in the mystery stories published around the turn of the century?

Both identifications presented obvious problems. Eustace Fraser Rawlins was a 'retired author' and enjoyed the support of all the most highly regarded works of reference. I could understand why those old stories written over thirty years before his death were not mentioned in his will. He was not a doctor, it is true, but an essential quality of any successful writer is the

combined with the group HOH. One of the most simple proteins we know is Lecithin. If this is hydrolised, one of the Amino-Acids produced is Choline from which Muscarine can be synthesised. The huge size of the protein molecule coupled with the complexity of its structure guarantees that there is always at least one asymmetrical Carbon Atom present, and consequently the protein molecule is invariably optically inactive. Muscarine, though a protein breakdown product, does not happen to contain an asymmetrical Carbon atom and is thus optically inactive.'

[1] 'My kind and eminent young friend has replied to your enquiry with promptitude. I enclose his notes and return yours that I sent him. He adds, "Haemophilia is an inherited condition confined wholly to the male sex, but transmitted only through the female line. Thus a male bleeder, marrying a normal woman, will produce male and female children who are perfectly normal. The children and all other descendants of the sons will be perfectly normal, though the male children of the daughters will be bleeders. This I have attempted to show in the enclosed table. Please let me know if it isn't absolutely clear and I will try to make it so". He has made some notes on your paper, and I hope these, with his notes, will clear up the points for you.'

ability to use a large library to provide himself with the information he needs. Some medical knowledge was displayed in the stories I have quoted, but not sufficient (I am professionally informed) to provide positive proof that one of the co-authors was a qualified physician. I confess, too, to being unimpressed by the distinct 'blood and thunder' element in these old stories of the 1890s, an opinion I think the reader may share if he is familiar with them. They are now hard to find, however, and it is of interest to record that of all the collaborations of Mrs L. T. Meade and Robert Eustace only *A Master of Mysteries* is now owned by the Leeds Library, founded in 1768 and now the oldest proprietary library in the British Isles. Sets of *The Strand Magazine* of the period are also very scarce today, probably because of the enthusiasm of collectors of the works of Sir Arthur Conan Doyle, many of which were serialised concurrently with the stories we are considering. I counted myself fortunate to find in a bookshop in Cartmel in Cumbria last autumn a battered volume of the *Strand* containing *The Brotherhood of the Seven Kings*, and another which included *Stories of the Sanctuary Club*. In the absence of access to the books and stories in full, I hope that the reader will find the sample of quotations I have included in this essay helpful.

Dr Eustace Robert Barton had no entry in *Who's Who*, and the facts I have gleaned about him have been extracted from *The Medical Directory* and the General Register Office in the main, together with one or two clues that were capable of being followed up in correspondence. He was born on 20 October 1868, and was the son of a physician, Dr Alfred Bowyer Barton and his wife Editha Helen formerly Howell. For some reason his birth was not registered by his father until 25 January 1869, over three months later. The birth address was an impressive one, being The Green, Hampton Court, Hampton. *Wibley's Directory* of the area for 1865 enlarges this address to 'A. Barton, M.D., The Green, North Side, Hampton Court'. Large-scale maps show this location as being a group of buildings known as 'Hampton Court House', occupied by Crown Tenants.

According to *The Medical Directory* Eustace Robert Barton followed his father into the profession of medicine, and qualified modestly as M.R.C.S., L.R.C.P. at University College in 1897.

He never obtained an M.D. degree. After qualifying, he seems to have lived in London for a few years, his address being 150 Cromwell Road. This was not the house of his father, who after leaving Hampton Court lived for some years in a large residence called Myskyns at Ticehurst in Sussex, afterwards moving to 8 Lexham Gardens, Kensington and finally to 7 Brechin Place, Kensington. By 1903, Eustace Robert Barton had moved to the Seamen's Hospital in Funchal, Madeira. In 1907 he was living (and presumably working) in Cintra in Portugal, where he remained for some years, returning to England to be shewn in *The Medical Directory* in 1914 as living at No. 6 Adelphi Road, Paignton, Devon. By 1916 he had moved to Ashton House, Harbury, Leamington Spa, which he left after two years to live at 'Grafton', Grafton Road, Torquay where he is shewn for the first time in *The Medical Directory* as 'Captain, R.A.M.C.'. He continued to use this title in every one of his entries until 1928. It was then changed rather oddly to 'Captain, late R.A.M.C.', this becoming a permanent feature of every remaining entry of Dr Barton in *The Medical Directory*.

He continued to live at 'Grafton' in Torquay until 1921, when he moved to St. Gwithians at Carbis Bay. His entries in *The Medical Directory* remained steady at this address until 1937 with the exception of the year 1928, when he is shown as living for some reason at Knill House, Treloyhan, St. Ives, Cornwall. In the 1937 entry Dr Barton was shown as '(Retired)', and having moved to Loft Studios, Norway Lane, St. Ives, this entry continuing without alteration until 1944 (we recall that he was living in Newport in 1943 and died there in that year) when the entry was altered to '(Retired). (Travelling)'. This entry was duplicated annually until 1950, when reference to him ceased seven years after his death.

These entries apart, I have ascertained from various sources that Dr Barton's life as a medical man, which was wandering and undistinguished, seems generally to have been limited to doing locums of a few months duration in various mental hospitals when the regular Medical Officer or Assistant Medical Officers were on leave. We remember that at his death in 1943 he was so engaged in a mental hospital in Newport. We recall that when he signed the collaboration agreement with Miss Sayers in

1929, he gave St. Andrew's Hospital, Northampton, as his address. I have been most fortunate in that Barton is still remembered by one person at St. Andrew's, which is a mental hospital and where Dr Barton worked, as always, in a temporary capacity. Mr A. G. Heritage, J.P., now the Administrative Officer, who would be a young man in Barton's day, wrote to me:

> He worked here many years ago, and I am quite sure that I am the only person at St. Andrew's who remembers him. He did not have a permanent appointment, but for a number of years acted as a locum tenens Medical Officer while some of our other doctors were away on annual holiday. I remember him being here in 1929, and for several years thereafter, but as he was not a member of the permanent staff I am afraid that we do not have any records which will give me exact dates. Certainly he was here during the summer of 1929, but his permanent address was Carbis Bay, Cornwall. He was quite a character, wore knee breeches and always a red tie, and was very much in the mould of a country doctor.

My friend Dr Eliot Slater, C.B.E., LL.D., who has given me generous help with the medical aspects of this inquiry, has told me that 'a locum tenens job in a county mental hospital was just about the softest snip in the whole of medicine, and would be just enough of a living for a man without ambition and defeated by the world'. Dr Slater gives some details of such an appointment on page 12 of his *Man, Mind and Heredity. Selected Papers of Eliot Slater on Psychiatry and Genetics* (Baltimore & London, 1971). One hour each morning in the wards and four afternoons off each week seems to have been a typical pattern. The two letters from Dr Barton to Miss Sayers to which I have referred in earlier pages were written from St. Gwithians and the County Mental Hospital at Gloucester. We recall that he wrote of the 'long leisure hours', the miserable spring spent at Carbis Bay and the locum tenens appointment at a mental hospital which he would fill until the autumn. The impression one gains from all this is that he only worked when the permanent staff were on annual leave. The picture of Dr Barton that emerges is that of an indolent man, who never settled down in general practice or in any permanent hospital appointment. His short periods of two years each at Paignton and Leamington Spa, followed by three years at Torquay, may have been spent in temporary appointments, unrecorded in *The Medical Directory*. He seems to have spent the First World War in England, joining the R.A.M.C. near the end of it. He seems to have clung proudly to his title of Captain to the end of his life.

As we have seen, Barton did not obtain his M.R.C.S. and L.R.C.P. at University College, London until 1897, so that he was nearly 30 when he qualified, which was late. In one of his letters to me Dr Eliot Slater suggests that Barton evidently enjoyed a carefree indolent youth, 'in no hurry to pass his exams and living on an allowance from a prosperous father. Even in my day at Cambridge and London we had a few perpetual students who went on from year to year and never got superannuated . . .' It was in 1897, the year in which Dr Barton finally passed his examinations, that we may assume that *The Brotherhood of the Seven Kings* and *A Master of Mysteries* were written by Robert Eustace in collaboration with L. T. Meade. We remember that the first of these titles was serialised in *The Strand Magazine*, commencing in January 1898, and that the second was published as a book in the same year. These were followed in rapid succession by *The Gold Star Line* in 1899, which was the same year in which *Stories of the Sanctuary Club* was published as a serial in *The Strand Magazine*, and as a book in 1900, all by L. T. Meade and Robert Eustace. *The Lost Square* and *The Sorceress of the Strand*, by the same authors, followed in 1902,[1] and in 1903 Robert Eustace collaborated with Gertrude Warden in publishing *The Stolen Pearl*. The impression given by this long string of titles, all written between the years 1897 and 1903, is one of continuous literary effort, which would not have been practicable for a young doctor in his year of qualification and those immediately following, when he would normally be expected to be devoted entirely to his profession, working hard in his first hospital appointment or as an assistant in a medical practice. I confess that in the early days of this investigation, when I was considering the bibliographical evidence in isolation, it did not seem to me that Eustace Robert Barton could possibly be the 'Robert Eustace' of those early years.

[1] In 1902 L. T. Meade and Robert Eustace also wrote three stories for *Pearson's Magazine* concerning 'Diana Marburge. The Oracle of Maddox Street'.

As the scope of the enquiry widened, however, it became obvious that other considerations must be taken into account. When the career of Dr Barton came under scrutiny, the evidence for any single-minded devotion to the profession of medicine was conspicuous by its absence. On the evidence of his entries in *The Medical Directory*, he never obtained a partnership in a medical practice or occupied any permanent position in a hospital. His wandering and undistinguished life seems to have alternated between long periods of leisure in boarding houses and temporary appointments in mental hospitals for a few months at a time when the permanent staff were on leave. The fact that he was so temporarily employed at the time of his death at the age of 75, leaving only £128 as his total fortune, tells its own sorry story of a miserably inadequate professional career in which Dr Barton did no more than manage to exist in the kind of life he had chosen.

Earlier in this essay I said that Sir Hugh Greene had suggested to me that an important addition to the history of detective fiction would be made if I could show which of the two Robert Eustaces had collaborated with Mrs L. T. Meade in the thrilling mystery stories published under their joint names around the turn of the century. The discoveries made in regard to both Eustace Fraser Rawlins and Eustace Robert Barton had made both men possibilities, but positive proof was still lacking. It was an interesting coincidence that the last of the seven early books with the name 'Robert Eustace' on the title-page was *The Stolen Pearl*, written with Gertrude Warden and published in 1903. It was in this year, we recall from his entries in *The Medical Directory*, that Dr Barton had left London and moved first to Funchal in Madeira and then to Cintra in Portugal.

It was at this point in the inquiry that it seemed to Sir Hugh Greene and myself that there was a single, last piece of evidence that might usefully be examined. It was the book, *A Human Bacillus. The Story of a Strange Character*, published in London by John Long. It was the only title, other than *The Hidden Treasures of Egypt*, which we know was the work of Eustace Fraser Rawlins, that was written by 'Robert Eustace' alone. The scarcity of the book is indicated by the fact that no copy is owned by the British Lending Library in Yorkshire, and that a copy I ultimately obtained and read came from the Cambridge University Library, bearing an acquisition stamp dated 1907, the year of publication. It was in mint condition, and had apparently never been read beyond the first few pages during the intervening seventy-two years. It was unopened (or 'uncut', as this condition is often imprecisely termed) after page 13. I opened the pages carefully to read the book, but left 13–16 unopened as I found them as a matter of historical record. The book is bound in red cloth with a pictorial top board and a gold lettered spine. It consists of 318 pages of text and 22 pages of advertisements of 'John Long's New and Forthcoming Books'. *A Human Bacillus* is without illustration.

The title-page settles for us the question that the author had been Mrs Meade's collaborator in earlier years. It reads 'A HUMAN BACILLUS/The/Story of a Strange Character/By/ Robert Eustace/*Part Author with L. T. Meade of "The Brother-hood of the/Seven Kings", "The Sanctuary Club", "The Sorceress/ of the Strand", "The Gold Star Line", "The Lost Square", etc. etc."*/London/John Long/Norris Street, Haymarket/(*All Rights Reserved*)'. The story concerns the lives of three close friends who have been at school together. It is told in the first person by Conrad Carlisle, a biologist, whose studies in Berlin and Vienna have caused the separation of the friends for some years. Jack Percival, after being up at Oxford, has inherited his father's estates in Wiltshire. The principal character, however, the 'Human Bacillus', is Dr Pedro Silver, a descendant of a noble Portuguese family resident in England for many years. Silver has been through 'one of the big London Schools of Medicine' and is an M.D. but does not practice. He makes a very great deal of money from research projects, however, and from writing. The following dialogue on pages 48–9 between Carlisle and Silver is of great interest because of its suggestion of a nostalgic recall of the collaboration with Mrs Meade. Silver points to his bookshelf:

> 'Write!', he echoed. 'Look at all this! Masses of it! What I can't use in fact I use in fiction. The usual detective stuff—and I'm very unpopular with Scotland Yard, I'm told, in consequence. Have you ever read any of them? "The Fraternity of the Six Princes", "The Mistress of Wonders", "The Chapel Club", "The Silver Planet

Navigation Society", "The Witch of Fleet Street", "The Discovered Circle", and many others. The main ideas and most of the writing is mine. I pass them on to my collaborator—they bring in cash for us both. I love doing them, they relieve me of a sort of phlegm of mental congestion. I am always boiling over with ideas, and welcome any channel of relief.'

Silver added that the books had 'made a sensation' with the public, but that he always 'used a "nom de plume" ' (because of his scientific reputation) on the title-pages coupled with the name of his co-author. The paragraph could almost be regarded as autobiographical, with the exception of the doubt aroused by his claim that he was responsible for the main ideas and most of the writing. Was this a piece of self-deception—an attempt to persuade himself that in different circumstances he could by his efforts alone have become a successful literary figure? Whatever the answer to that question may be, there can be no doubt that the Robert Eustace who wrote *A Human Bacillus* in 1907 had been L. T. Meade's collaborator in earlier years. The question still to be resolved was whether he was Eustace Fraser Rawlins or Eustace Robert Barton.

In my convinced opinion, he was Dr Barton. I say this for two reasons based on the text of *A Human Bacillus*, the first being geographical. The story involves limited foreign travel by the main characters, and Chapter VIII (page 147) opens with the following:

> There are few scenes more impressive and beautiful than the approach to the Bay of Funchal in early morning. As we went on deck soon after daybreak the following day, we found that we had already passed the outlying island of Porta Santo, and were rounding the eastern point of Madeira, a tongue of sharp crags, upon which stands the São Lorenzo light-house. On our left lay the three Deserta Islands. . . . A few moments more and we had rounded the point of the Brazen Head, when the full beauty of Funchal Bay burst upon our view.

On page 148 the attractions of 'the little town of Funchal' are almost lyrically described.

We recall from Dr Barton's entries in *The Medical Directory* that in 1903 he moved from London to the Seaman's Hospital in Funchal, and that by 1907 he was living in Cintra in Portugal, these being his only foreign addresses recorded in the directory.

We may think that it can scarcely be a coincidence that these are the only two foreign place-names that play any part in the story of *A Human Bacillus*. Chapter XIII opens with the sentences:

> We arrived at the Rocio Station at Lisbon on Saturday morning, where we were met by an agent into whose hands the whole of the arrangements for the transportation of ourselves and our baggage to Cintra had been entrusted.

The following passages occurs on pages 301–2:

> I shall never forget my first joyous impressions of Cintra that exquisite morning. To arrive there, after passing through the dreary, uninteresting country that separates it from the capital is like entering some cool green oasis set in a desert land.

This is followed by four pages of detailed description of the beauties of Cintra. I have no doubt in my mind, at least, that these graphical and precise descriptions of the attractions of Funchal and Cintra, where Dr Barton lived for some years, are nostalgic and personal.

The second point of interest and value in the identification of Dr Barton provided by the text of *A Human Bacillus* is the display of medical knowledge, obviously more convincing than the smatterings of information contained in the collaborations of the 1890s, and reflecting the experience obtained during his temporary appointments in the interim. The principal case described (pp. 54 ff.) in which Dr Silver's scientific expertise is brought into the case as a last resort is that of loss of memory over a period of seven years by an elderly man suffering from a form of dementia not sufficiently serious to warrant admission to an asylum. Silver's theory, which in the book proves to be successful, is that the 'loss of memory might be due to sluggish metabolism of the cerebral tissues' and that 'in feverish conditions the metabolism of all the tissues of the body are enormously increased—the brain tissue, of course, being included'. By an injection of serum Dr Silver induces a feverish condition in the patient by raising his temperature to $105°$. The old gentleman regains his memory, and is able instantly to recall the whereabouts of his missing will. The interesting and significant point of this incident is that when Silver describes to Carlisle the research he carried out on the pathology of dementia, on which he relied for the success of the experiment just described, he asserts that he gained no help from medical literature. 'Then I visited and corresponded with the medical officers attached to our big asylums'. It was these gentlemen, experienced and practical, from whom Dr Silver said that he obtained the case histories on which his successful research was based.

If we think that *A Human Bacillus* is a document of psychological significance, throwing light on the character of its author and the kind of man he would have liked to have been, then we may be tempted to link his justification of the importance of medical officers in mental hospitals with the claim that in his literary work Dr Silver was responsible for the ideas of the books he wrote in collaboration, and for most of the actual writing. It is of additional interest, we may think, that the story of *A Human Bacillus* ends with the suicide of Dr Silver.

I have made the effort to solve the mystery of 'Robert Eustace' for two reasons, the first of which has been accomplished. We now know that although the *British Museum Catalogue* and other highly regarded sources of bibliographical information attribute all the recorded writings of 'Robert Eustace' to Eustace Fraser Rawlins, the latter gentleman was only responsible for the entry *The Hidden Treasures of Egypt*, published in 1925. With that exception, I think the case is proved that 'Robert Eustace' was the pseudonym of Dr Robert Eustace Barton. The second reason I undertook the enquiry was because of my perplexity over Dorothy L. Sayers' treatment of Dr Barton in the publication of *Have His Carcase* in 1932. We recall that in 1928 she included two short stories in which he was involved in the first Gollancz collection that she edited. In 1930 his name appeared with hers as joint author of *The Documents in the Case*. Admittedly the information about muscarine he obtained from his 'young friend' at Oxford was shown to be inaccurate, and Miss Sayers admitted it in print. We must concede, however, that neither she nor her subsequent publishers, Victor Gollancz Ltd, thought it necessary to add any note on the matter to later editions of the book, which is still in print today. The mistake is not mentioned in either of the two existing biographies of Miss Sayers, nor in the *Annotated Guide* to her work by Mr Harmon and Miss Burger.

The difference between her treatment of Barton in *The Documents in the Case* and *Have His Carcase* was remarkable, bearing in mind that she had relied upon him to obtain the information she needed about haemophilia to write the second book, and that the details he supplied from his 'kind and eminent young friend' at Edinburgh University were accurate and remarkably clear. Her total absence of any acknowledgment of this willing and excellent help in the writing of *Have His Carcase* is startling enough by itself, we may think. Her grateful thanks on the verso of the title-page to 'Mr John Rhode, who gave me generous help with all the hard bits', however, must have come as a bitter blow to Dr Barton. We cannot think that Miss Sayers would not be fully aware of this consequence.

In her article in *The Listener* at the beginning of 1932 Miss Sayers did not blame her collaborator for the mistake. She said that they had consulted experts, who had proved to be wrong, in a matter that was admitted to be complicated. She and Dr Barton were in friendly correspondence about haemophilia as late as June 1931 to my knowledge. I have never heard it suggested that Miss Sayers was a spiteful person, who would, as it were, wreak vengeance on Dr Barton by ignoring him completely in *Have His Carcase*, and make matters worse by recording her thanks to another writer. I believe, therefore, that there must be another explanation for this curious incident, an incident upon which no writer upon Miss Sayers has ever commented to the best of my knowledge.

The only alternative solution that occurs to me is that between June 1931 and the publication of *Have His Carcase* in 1932, in which the insertion of a small amount of print on the verso of the title-page could be a late operation, some information about Dr Barton reached Miss Sayers that shocked her, and caused her to dissociate herself from him forthwith. I may be wholly wrong in considering that Dr Barton was a homosexual, which in 1931 would result in social ostracism, in marked contrast with the permissive benevolence with which it is regarded today. The facts that so far as we know he never married, and that in his will he left everything he possessed to a young man with whom he was on friendly terms prove nothing in themselves. On the other hand, the positive documentary proof that Barton's father regarded his son with contemptuous dislike must have some fairly drastic explanation.

Dr Alfred Bowyer Barton was a distinguished man of energy and ability. Having qualified as an M.R.C.S. in 1847 he obtained the successive appointments of principal Surgeon to the Royal West Indies Steam Co. from 1848 to 1853, to be followed by a similar position with the Pacific and Orient Co. from 1853 to 1857. I fancy that he must have been possessed of some inherited wealth to enable him, after only four years work in England, to undertake in 1861 the exploration of the Yangtsze-Kiang, in company with Major-General Sarel, C.B., 17th Lancers and Captain Blakiston, R.A., together with an interpreter, four Sikhs of the 11th Punjab Rifles and four Chinese servants. In a lecture delivered to the Royal Geographical Society on 24 March 1862 Dr Barton said that the objective of this expedition was to follow the course of the great river of China to the province of Sz'chuan, and then to march from its capital Ching-tu over the lofty mountains skirting the western border of China and so to Lassa. The journey would continue along the northern slopes of the Himalaya range to Lake Mansorawa, striking the road across the Himalayas into the plains of North-West India, a distance of about 4000 miles.

Dr Barton's interest in the East was life-long, and we notice that as late as October 1894 he contributed an article to *The Times* 'On the Outlook for China'. This interest, however, did not prevent him from pursuing his medical career with vigour and success. After his return to England in 1862 he must have renewed his studies with determination, for in 1865 he obtained his F.R.C.S. by examination, and received his M.D. degree at St Andrews University in 1866. By 1868 at latest he was installed in his house at Hampton Court, where Eustace Robert Barton was born in October of that year, and registered by his father in January 1869.

Dr Alfred Bowyer Barton, who was to die in 1905, signed his will on 14 November 1900. It was a long and complicated document, appointing three Trustees to deal with his large fortune, which was vested in them and did not rank for estate duty, and was ultimately to be divided equally between his three children Edwin Alfred, Hubert Howell and Ethel Sarel.

The amount of money involved must have been considerable, since his personal estate, which attracted probate, was valued at over £25,000. His third son, Eustace Robert, was left nothing except an anuity of £120 per annum, payable quarterly and commencing three months after his father's death. This was subject to the strict proviso that should any event occur that would result in Eustace's small annuity becoming vested in some other person then payment would cease 'as if he were dead'. It seems impossible to place any interpretation upon this proviso other than that Eustace was indulging in some association of which his father violently disapproved.

The first codicil was signed on 30 July 1902 and was solely concerned with Eustace's annuity, mainly but not wholly in connexion with a technical point probably raised by the solicitors. The sum of £4,000 was vested in the Trustees, and the annuity was to be the interest on this sum, which at the average rate of those days of 3% would amount to about £120. The other alterations were wholly to Eustace's disadvantage. If he should assign, charge or otherwise dispose of some part of the income, or become bankrupt, then he would cease to receive it and the £4,000 would form part of the residuary estate and be inherited by the other three children.

The second and last codicil, signed on 25 June 1903, was entirely directed towards the further discomfiture of Eustace. The clauses relating to the annuity in the will and first codicil were repeated and confirmed. The codicil continued, 'Now I hereby declare that in addition to such events as mentioned in my first codicil my Trustees shall cease to pay the income of the settled legacy to my said son who now resides abroad [Eustace was living in Funchal in 1903, we recall] if without the written consent of my Trustees he returns to or sets foot in the United Kingdom and the trust in his favour shall thereupon determine'. It seems abundantly clear that Alfred Bowyer Barton never wished to see his son Eustace again, and in fact never did. As we have seen, Eustace did not return to England until long after his father's death. Whether the Trustees gave him permission, and so allowed him to retain the pittance provided by his father I do not know.

Estrangements between parents and children are common

enough nowadays, sad to say, thanks to the decline in moral standards and the frequent cold indifference of the young towards the elderly. This was unusual at the turn of the century, however, when families were closely knit and children regarded their parents with loyalty and affection. The sad conclusion it seems impossible to avoid is that Eustace Robert Barton had mortally offended his father in some way before 1900, the date of the original will. While it is true that Eustace seems to have shown a lack of enthusiasm for his father's profession, and to have devoted the vital years following his qualification in 1897 to writing a series of sensational mystery stories in collaboration with Mrs L. T. Meade instead of diligently pursuing his medical career, I find it most difficult to believe that this could have been sufficient reason by itself for his father's implacable hostility and complete scorn, manifested in a will and two codicils and lasting for at least five years, and in effect repudiating Eustace as a member of the family. As I have remarked, the second codicil makes it clear that his father never wished to see Eustace's face again. Some edisode involving Eustace in a homosexual affair in the years following the imprisonment of Oscar Wilde in 1895 and discovered by his father, would doubtless have produced such a result.

If we think that *A Human Bacillus* is to some extent autobiographical, and we attach importance to the fact that it was written and published in 1907, two years after the death of Eustace's father, then we may think that the fact that its gloomy pages end with the self-destruction of Dr Silver is not without significance. It was the only book that Dr Barton wrote alone, and its pages are therefore worthy of scrutiny for clues to the personality of a very odd character. On pages 289–90 is a description of Dr Silver by Professor Rich, a consultant in a teaching hospital, in conversation with Silver's friend Carlisle:

> He was a queer fellow, Silver, in those days—a brilliant genius, as I knew well—and in many ways a charming and most fascinating man, but I don't think that his influence on any young man would have been a desirable one. Of course, you must know more than I about that, for you were all boys together.

Whatever his shortcomings may have been, Eustace Robert

Barton seems to have suffered for them, for it cannot be imagined that his life was a happy one. He seems to have loved Cornwall, where he lived on and off for many years. Mr A. G. Heritage, we recall, said that his permanent address was Carbis Bay, where he had lived since 1921. In 1937, *The Medical Directory* showed that he had 'retired' and moved to St. Ives, which was close at hand in Cornwall. It must have been a miserable end to his life to have to move to Newport in Wales, with only £128 in the world, to die in his last temporary employment as an assistant medical officer in a mental hospital at the age of 75. That he was a lonely man, as homosexuals are said to be, would seem to be demonstrated by the fact that his death was not noticed in *The Medical Directory* and that his entry continued for another six years. He can scarcely be regarded as a success as a medical man, while in the literary field only his pseudonym of Robert Eustace is remembered, and all his work attributed in standard works of reference to Eustace Fraser Rawlins. I hope that this, at least, has been corrected in this essay.

How and where he met Dorothy L. Sayers I do not know. It is possible that when she felt that collaboration would be needed to write *The Documents in the Case* she sought him out, knowing that Dr Edgar Beaumont had died in 1922. As she had included the short story, 'The Tea-Leaf', by Edgar Jepson and Robert Eustace, published as late as 1925, in the collection she edited for Victor Gollancz in 1928, and would have needed to obtain permission to reprint it, she would doubtless have Dr Barton's name and address in her files. Whether the theory in this essay for her failure to acknowledge the help he gave her in regard to haemophilia in *Have His Carcase* is well-founded or not, their acquaintance seems to have been of short duration. It is of interest that after the publication of *The Documents in the Case*, Dr Barton wrote nothing more so far as I am aware.[1]

---

[1] Since this book went into page-proof I have learnt, through the kindness of Sir Hugh Greene who made the discovery in a bookseller's catalogue, that a story by Edgar Jepson and Robert Eustace, 'ALL SQUARE', was published in *Pearson's Monthly*, September, 1936.

VIII

THE DATES OF BUSMAN'S HONEYMOON

Iɴ 'The Dates in *The Red-Headed League*', one of her four Baker Street essays in *Unpopular Opinions*, Dorothy L. Sayers clarified for us some of the chronological anomalies in Sir Arthur Conan Doyle's second short story about Sherlock Holmes, published in *The Strand Magazine* in August 1891. The task to which Miss Sayers applied her enthusiasm and analytical skill was one before which earlier investigators had quailed, and not without reason. There were obvious difficulties, for example, in reconciling the contradictory statements in Dr Watson's story that the Red-Headed League was disbanded on 9 October, 1890, 'just two months' after its advertisement in the *Morning Chronicle* of 27 April in the same year. The fact that Miss Sayers overcame these and other difficulties in dating the affair of *The Red-Headed League* has tempted me to believe that a note on the problems inherent in the history of the play and the book, *Busman's Honeymoon*, may be of interest.

Before we examine some of the more sophisticated questions posed by *Busman's Honeymoon*, it should perhaps be said that Mrs Janet Hitchman's date of 1938 for Victor Gollancz's first London edition of the book in her 'The Works of Dorothy L. Sayers, 1893–1957'[1] is a year too late. The year of publication, 1937, is on the title-page of *Busman's Honeymoon. A Love Story with Detective Interruptions*, which is before me as I write. To this dating we may add the fact that *The English Catalogue of*

---

[1] *Such a Strange Lady* (London, 1975), pp. 201–3.

Books tells us that the month of publication of the first London edition was June 1937.

A much more serious published error (by reason of its provenance) that has caused some confusion, this time in *The British Museum General Catalogue of Printed Books*, a work of reference usually regarded as impeccably authoritative, concerns the play. I have the second impression of the latter publication in my collection. The title-page reads, 'Dorothy L. Sayers and M. St. Clare Byrne/BUSMAN'S HONEYMOON/*A Detective Comedy in Three Acts*/LONDON/VICTOR GOLLANCZ LTD 1939'. On the centre of the verso of the title-page is printed '*First published February 1937/Second impression March 1939*'. The date of the first edition of the play is confirmed by *The English Catalogue of Books*. To the evidence that the play preceded the book we may add the dedication of the novel on page [7] to Miss Sayers' friends Muriel St Clare Byrne, Helen Simpson and Marjorie Barber. In the second paragraph Miss Say.ers wrote:

> You, Muriel, were in sort a predestined victim, since you wrote with me the play to which this novel is but the limbs and outward flourishes: my debt and your long-sufferings are all the greater.

It may be thought that the sequence of events is clear. Yet the entry for the play in column 1013 of volume 213 of *The British Museum General Catalogue of Printed Books* states firmly and incorrectly that the play, '1937. 8°' by 'Sayers (Dorothy L.) and Byrne (M. St. C.)' was 'Based on the novel by D. L. Sayers'.

Another matter that is capable of agreeable amplification and discussion is the printed statement on page [6] of the published play that *Busman's Honeymoon* was first presented by Mr Anmer Hall at the Comedy Theatre, London, on Wednesday, 16 December 1936. This was a traditionally correct statement of the date of the West End opening of the play. Thanks to the generous gift to me by my friend Wilfrid Scott-Giles of a collection of Sayers documents now virtually unobtainable, I am able additionally to record the details of the earlier provincial presentation of the play, and to quote from the reviews of both that and the later London opening. I am in a position to describe one *contretemps* that is certainly worthy of record. Friends experienced in theatre affairs tell me that the fact that the play was performed some months before it was available in printed form is perfectly normal and commonplace.

The evidence in my collection and the availability of *The English Catalogue* seemed to make the sequence of events reasonably clear. The play was written by Dorothy L. Sayers and Muriel St Clare Byrne in collaboration at a date and in circumstances to be discussed, in time to be produced and performed late in 1936, and was printed and published in February 1937. The 'limbs and outward flourishes' that were additionally necessary to enable it to be transformed into a novel were added, and the book, written by Dorothy L. Sayers alone, was published by Victor Gollancz in June 1937. All this seemed perfectly straightforward, but for two discoveries made within a few weeks of each other.

First, in his 'Contribution Toward a Bibliography of Dorothy L. Sayers', published in the *Bulletin of Bibliography* of May–August 1944, James Sandoe wrote:

> The novel was published in England in June, 1937; but Harcourt, Brace brought out the American edition of the novel in February, 1937.

In connexion with this first point, it is of interest to record that Wilfrid Scott-Giles has a copy of the first American edition of *Busman's Honeymoon*, published by Harcourt, Brace and Company of New York and presented to him by Dorothy L. Sayers. It has 381 pages, as opposed to the 446 pages of the first English edition, an important difference evidently unknown to Robert B. Harmon and Margaret A. Burger. On page 9 of their *An Annotated Guide to the Works of Dorothy L. Sayers*, they describe both the English and American editions of 1937 as having 381 pages.

The second discovery was that in 1976 I added a rare item to my Sayers collection. It was a set of bound page-proofs in paper wrappers of the Gollancz first edition of the novel, *Busman's Honeymoon*, with the title-page repeated on the front wrapper. Type-setting errors apart, these proofs are identical with the first English edition with the exception of two points of difference. First, on the final page 446, the 11-line quotation of

John Donne's *Eclogue for the Marriage of the Earl of Somerset*, with which the book closes, follows the final six lines of the text proper of the novel at the top of the same page. In the first London edition of the book, the *Eclogue* has been moved from page 446 to the centre of the un-numbered facing page, the recto of the last and eighth leaf of the final gathering of the book. It is of the greatest interest to record that in Wilfrid Scott-Giles' copy of the first American edition the *Eclogue* follows the text on the final page, precisely as in the English page-proofs. On the occasion of the presentation of the book to Mr Scott-Giles, Miss Sayers drew his attention to this, marking the proposed alteration in pencil, with the comment that it was her firm intention that in the finished book John Donne's *Eclogue* should have the distinction of a page to itself.

The second point of interest in the English page-proofs is that they are dated 1936 on the title-page. I fancy that two reasonable inferences can be made from this evidence, the first being that the proofs were in print by December 1936 at latest. I based the second deduction on my experiences with the publishers and printers of my own books. I believe that for the novel to have proceeded through galley-proofs to page proofs by December 1936 at latest means that the typescript must have been completed and sent to Victor Gollancz in the late summer of that year on the tightest of schedules. It had become apparent that the sequence of events was not quite so straightforward as I had supposed.

I am much indebted to Miss Muriel St Clare Byrne for throwing light on the history of the writing of the play. A version of the story was published in the *Evening Standard* of 5 November, 1936, apparently as a result of an interview with Miss Sayers some twenty months after the event. The article, 'LORD PETER WIMSEY TO TAKE THE STAGE', was written by Stephen Williams:

> Miss Dorothy L. Sayers called one morning on an old friend of hers, Miss M. St Clare Byrne. 'How are you?' said Miss Byrne. 'Terrible,' said Miss Sayers. 'I've had the chimney-sweep in the house this morning.' And she whereupon entertained her friend to a pantomimic representation of the sweep's methods as he attempted to insert his body into the chimney.

'Splendid,' said Miss Byrne; 'there's an ideal opening to a play.' 'But I don't want to write a play,' said Miss Sayers; 'I can't start learning to write a new technique.' 'Well, we'll write it together,' said Miss Byrne.

So they did. The result is 'Busman's Honeymoon', which opens in Birmingham next week, and comes to the West End (they hope) before Christmas. It is (of course) a detective play, and forms a kind of sequel to the novel *Gaudy Night*. It is *not*, however, a dramatisation of any of Miss Sayers' novels. All the familiar characters are there, nevertheless. Mr Dennis Arundell will play Lord Peter, Mr Norman V. Norman Bunter, and Miss Veronica Turleigh Harriet.

'There are, I think, two original features about this play,' Miss Sayers told me. 'Every movement is done, every clue is laid, in full sight of the audience, so that the audience has as much chance as the crime investigator of solving the problem. There are no red herrings, and there is no funny business behind the scenes. Then, the "love interest", so painfully extraneous in plays of this kind, is here an essential part of the theme. Lord Peter is involved in criminal investigation during his honeymoon'.

According to Miss Byrne, the idea of the collaboration in the writing of the play began in February 1935. Some time before that date Miss Byrne, who among other distinctions listed in *Who's Who* was a lecturer at the Royal Academy of Dramatic Art for over twelve years, had declined a commission from a well-known theatrical producer to write a play featuring the Sayers characters. Miss Sayers, on the other hand, had no professional experience of the theatre at all at this time. Her later distinction in this field of literary activity was to come, and it therefore seems to me to be of the greatest interest to be able to pin-point the date of the start of her enthusiasm and success in this sphere of work. Thanks to Miss St Clare Byrne's diary entries and her admirably clear memory, the facts of the partnership have been made available to me.

Miss Sayers came to Miss Byrne's home in St. John's Wood on 10 February 1935 for the first discussion of the proposed play, a discussion that extended into the small hours. The project was planned in more detail over lunch at Rules on the following day. It was agreed that Miss Sayers, who by this time had the outline of the plot clearly in her mind, should draft the first of the proposed three acts as a preliminary, despite her lack of professional knowledge of the theatre. It was quickly completed by her, and Miss Byrne then worked over the draft for three weeks, which included a week-end spent at Miss Sayers' home in Witham, Essex in late February. Further extensive working sessions followed, including another week-end stay in Witham on 21–3 March.

The play was not finished until the end of the summer of 1935, when attempts were made to place it with a London management. Maurice Brown was very interested in the play, and retained it for some months. It was not until January 1936 at earliest, however, according to Miss Byrne's recollection, that he found the backing he needed was unfortunately not available. This caused a hiatus in the placing of the play, and it was not until August 1936 that Anmer Hall wired to Miss Byrne, who was on holiday in Devon at the time, to say that he definitely wished to produce *Busman's Honeymoon*.

The generous gift to me by Wilfrid Scott-Giles of his collection of the programmes and reviews of the play enable me to be exact in my recording of its first presentation, since I have before me the printed programme of the Birmingham Theatre Royal for the week beginning Monday, 9 November 1936, a page of which is reproduced as the frontispiece of this book. It will be noticed that it was signed by both authors as a souvenir of the occasion, thus adding to its value and interest as a collector's item. The play was well received, and it is a pleasure to reproduce its first review in the *Birmingham Gazette* of 10 November 1936:

FIRST PRODUCTION OF NEW DETECTIVE COMEDY.
'BUSMAN'S HONEYMOON'
AT THE ROYAL.

When a critic can sit in a theatre and almost entirely forget that he has a task to perform when he leaves it, you may depend upon it that the show, to say the least, is of exceptional quality.

One can make that assertion without any reserve whatsoever about 'Busman's Honeymoon', the new detective comedy which is being presented this week at the Birmingham Royal Theatre prior to London production. Both as a detective thriller and as a comedy it is a play of distinction.

So far as the crime story is concerned—well, if there has been staged a more interesting plot, more dramatically presented and more neatly unravelled, I haven't seen it. The crime in 'Busman's Honeymoon' has the advantage of most crime in real life that it is really convincing. And there are no loose ends.

That, of course, was to be expected since Miss Dorothy Sayers, one of our best and most workmanlike of crime story writers, is joint authoress with M. St. Clare Byrne. But, in addition, we are also presented to a little gallery of characters so rich in personality and so cleverly drawn that the play has appeal as a comedy solely, even though one may not be particularly interested in the sport and science of detection.

The hero of 'Busman's Honeymoon' is Miss Dorothy Sayers' celebrated amateur sleuth, Lord Peter Wimsey, who (readers of the Wimsey crime books will be glad to know) is now safely married to his Harriet Vane. And one pays the highest possible tribute to the acting of Dennis Arundell and Veronica Turleigh, who respectively enact those rôles, when one asserts that no admirer of these two fictional characters is likely to be disappointed in seeing them in the flesh. Their performances are highly admirable.

And if, to some extent, they are over-shadowed by two other pieces of real acting it is because in the voluble Mrs Ruddle and the twittery Miss Twitterton, the playwrights present two characters of marked personality who are portrayed by two actresses of great comedic ability. The studies of Nellie Bowman as Mrs Ruddle and Christine Silver as Miss Twitterton are brilliant.

But every part is well done—as befits a play which is truly outstanding in its artistry and entertainment value. W. H. B.

The *Birmingham Post* was equally enthusiastic, saying that Wimsey, Harriet and Bunter were 'even better company on the stage than they were in Miss Sayers' well-known novel *Gaudy Night*', and adding that 'this is as good a play as we have seen for some time. It is sound and exciting; it arouses interest at curtain rise, and maintains it to the end.'

The play was repeated at Brighton during the following week, and at one other South Coast theatre before its London opening at the Comedy Theatre on Wednesday, 16 December 1936. The cast was precisely the same as that of the Birmingham production. I have in my collection the Comedy Theatre programme, and reviews of 17 December, 1936 in *The Times*, the *Daily Telegraph*, the *Morning Post*, the *Daily Mail*, the *Daily Sketch*

and the *News Chronicle*. All (with one exception) were con-
sistently favourable, the *Morning Post* calling it 'gay but
thrillsome detective comedy, cleverly written, brilliantly acted
and enthusiastically received', but regrettably adding, 'It would
be a shame to give away the secret, but those who want to guess
should watch the pot of cactus in the middle of the stage.'

George Buchanan in the *News Chronicle*, in a notice lacking
enthusiasm, broke the rules of dramatic criticism still further by
hinting strongly at the *modus operandi* of the murder of Noakes:

> The closing scene where a brass pot of cactus suspended from the
> ceiling is swung across the stage, smashing a lamp, is exciting
> theatre. I was sorry we had not more ingenious action such as this,
> and less of the interminable asking of questions.

By contrast, the reviewer in the *Birmingham Post* had been
careful to remark:

> There can be no detailed discussion of the plot. With a detective
> play it is not done. But it is no betrayal of confidence to say that the
> murder of Mr Noakes is efficiently executed, and as efficiently
> detected with all Lord Peter's usual skill.

The first two sentences of this very proper comment formed the
theme of the letter to the Editor of the *News Chronicle* written
by Wilfrid Scott-Giles on 17 December, 1936:

> Sir,
> Does not professional etiquette enjoin upon a dramatic
> critic, especially of a detective play, a strict reticence regarding the
> dénoument of the plot? Yet your critic, in his account of 'Busman's
> Honeymoon', gives so strong a hint of the solution of the mystery as
> to spoil a good play for all who read his review. In this he puts
> himself in a class with that infuriating nuisance, the talkative person
> who has seen the play before, and insists on telling his companion,
> and everyone else within earshot, exactly what is going to happen
> next.
>
> Yours, etc.,
C. W. Scott-Giles.

And so the play was launched. According to James Sandoe, it
made its first American appearance on 12–17 July 1937 at West-
chester Playhouse, Mt. Kisco, New York, and was reviewed in

the *New York Times* of 13 July, 1937. The fact that it was a financial success is recorded by Muriel St Clare Byrne, who has written that the production of the play gave Miss Sayers 'money and to spare for the first time'. In 1940 it was made into a film by Metro-Goldwyn-Mayer British Studios Ltd, with Robert Montgomery and Constance Cummings as Peter and Harriet, but the authors disapproved of the presentation. It has appeared as a B.B.C. television play in 1947, 1949, 1957 and 1965.

On the question of the priority of the play Miss St Clare Byrne has written:

> When Dorothy started the novel she had definitely warned her publisher that in no circumstances whatsoever could it be published before the play was produced, and I seem to remember that he was not particularly pleased with this arrangement. But she was absolutely firm, and described the situation in the Dedicatory Note. But there is no question as to the priority of the novel. She did not begin working on it until the play was being offered to the London managements. . . . I can quite understand that the proofs of the novel are dated 1936, but there is no question, and never has been any, of the novel being even considered as a possibility until after the play was written.

We know from the earlier account by Miss Byrne that the play was finished at the end of the summer of 1935, which gives us the first date when Miss Sayers could have considered writing the novel. The hiatus in the acceptance of the play by a London management followed, and through circumstances outside the control of the authors nearly a year elapsed before Anmer Hall sent his telegram to Miss Byrne. I fancy that this unexpected delay is the reason why the page-proofs of the novel were ready sufficiently early to be dated 1936. In parenthesis, it is of interest to notice that according to the MS. of the novel preserved in the Marion E. Wade Collection at Wheaton College, Illinois, the original title of the book was to have been *Busman's Honeymoon. A Murder Theme with Sentiment*. From a three-page 'authors note' in the same place, we learn that at some stage there was the possibility that Miss Byrne's participation in the writing of the play might have been concealed under the pseudonym 'M. St Clove Bylue'.

We can understand Miss Sayers' reason for not wishing

Victor Gollancz to publish *Busman's Honeymoon* as a novel until the play had established itself. On the other hand, to my mind it seems a little hard on Gollancz, who had the page-proofs ready in 1936 but respected his author's wish, that Harcourt, Brace and Co. of New York were able to publish the book four months before the English edition, with the John Donne *Eclogue* in a position of which the author disapproved. Gollancz, as we have seen, corrected the proof, and the London edition was as Miss Sayers wished.

IX

DOROTHY L. SAYERS AND
PSYCHICAL RESEARCH

In 'Denver Ducis: The Power and the Glory', the second of
the three parts of the *Epithalamion* of *Busman's Honeymoon*,
we are told of the circumstances in which the newly-wedded
Harriet (or Lady Peter Wimsey as she was now) paid her first
visit to Bredon Hall at Denver Ducis (or Duke's Denver) in
Norfolk. After the arrest of Crutchley for the murder of Mr
Noakes at Great Pagford in Hertfordshire as a result of
Wimsey's investigation of the case during his honeymoon, the
amende honorable of a journey to London had been made to see
Sir Impey Biggs after a late sitting of the House, to retain him
for the defence. Aware from experience of the likely cure for her
husband's state of restlessness and mental exhaustion at the end
of a case, Harriet had agreed with his suggestion that they
should set off in the small hours to drive the ninety miles from
London to Bredon Hall, about fifteen miles west of Downham
Market, to arrive in time for hot baths, breakfast and a few
hours of much needed sleep.

That afternoon, his equanimity restored, Peter began to show
his wife over the great house, with 'nothing before Queen
Elizabeth', and 'specimens of all the bad periods since then and
one or two of the good ones'. After the portrait gallery of
Wimsey ancestors had been inspected, Peter suggested that
Harriet should see the library, 'full of the most appalling rubbish,
and the good stuff isn't properly catalogued'. As Peter unex-

pectedly had to attend to some estate business in the absence of his brother the Duke, he suggested that Harriet might like to look round the library, and that he would join her as soon as he could. He added that she might find Matthew, his third cousin, 'not the one who's potty and lives at Nice, his younger brother', working in the library. Apparently Matthew Wimsey, harmless, shy and slightly deaf, had been engaged to restore order to the library within his limitations of short-sightedness, an entire lack of method and an inability to keep to one subject at a time, in exchange for his keep.

Harriet found the library rather dark (it was late afternoon) but restful, with its 'sweet, musty odour of ancient books'. On the large library table, deep in books and papers, she found traces of Cousin Matthew's work—a half-written sheet of what appeared to be a family history in an elderly man's hand-writing and an open manuscript book of household expenses for the year 1587. Turning the corner of the bookshelves, she was startled momentarily to see an elderly gentleman, standing by the window with a book in his hand. He was grey-haired and slightly bald, and was wearing a dressing gown. In the certainty that he must be Cousin Matthew, Harriet said that she was Peter's wife. The figure smiled, with a slight wave of the hand, as if indicating that she should make herself at home. Harriet assumed that his disinclination for conversation was explained by his deafness and shyness, and continued her tour of the library. Five minutes later, she noticed that he had moved, and was now looking down at her from the top of a little staircase that led to the gallery. At that moment Peter came into the library, switching on the electric lights as he did so, with the remark, 'All in the dark, lady? I'm sorry to have been so long. Come and have tea'.

At tea in the Blue Room, Harriet was introduced to Matthew Wimsey, a slight, oldish man, dressed in an old-fashioned knicker-bocker suit, with a thin grey beard and spectacles. When she described her experience in the library, she was told she had seen the ghost of 'Old Gregory', a cousin of the Duke of Denver in the reign of William and Mary, and had been most fortunate to do so. Cousin Matthew Wimsey described an experience of his own when he had been a percipient of the apparition, which he had disturbed in the fourth bay when taking the Bredon Letters from the shelf. The figure had vanished. Peter explained that neither his brother Gerald, the present Duke, nor his wife Helen, had enjoyed any similar experiences of seeing 'Old Gregory'.

What are we to make of this ghost story by Miss Sayers, introduced by her into the penultimate chapter of her last novel? What light does it throw upon her attitude towards the alleged supernatural, and her knowledge of what is popularly known as 'psychical research', or sometimes more grandly today as 'parapsychology'? How closely was she acquainted with the vast literature that has proliferated around this controversial subject, more especially since the foundation of the Society for Psychical Research in 1882? Did she believe in ghosts and the possibility of communication with the dead? In the case of Dorothy L. Sayers, a devout Christian and a woman of acute intelligence and considerable education, these questions seem to me to be of the greatest interest. As the subject has not been discussed by any previous writer about Miss Sayers, I have thought it of interest to examine some of the clues in her novels that bear upon the matter, of which the apparition of 'Old Gregory' is not the only example.

The fact that through the centuries, persons in normal physical and mental health have had experiences which they call 'seeing a ghost' is as certain as that other persons have had hallucinations when under the influence of alcohol, drugs or morbid mental states. I do not think that this can be denied by anyone who is capable of understanding the nature of historical evidence. The *interpretation* may be erroneous: the *experience* is certain. What also seems to be thoroughly established by the mass of recorded testimony available to the student is that the experience of 'seeing a ghost' by a normal person is exceedingly rare: perhaps once in a lifetime. Thus we notice that Harriet's life before she visited Bredon Hall for the first time, as recorded by Miss Sayers in the four novels that concern her, had not been disturbed by previous 'hauntings'. She believed that the figure she saw in the library was Cousin Matthew, and that the commonsense explanation of the fact that he did not speak to her was his known deafness and extreme shyness.

Another point that convinces me that Miss Sayers knew what

she was writing about is the anecdote of the real Cousin Matthew, told over the tea-cups after Peter and Harriet had joined the party in the Blue Room. According to him, he had also seen an apparition, but no description of the figure is given, so that we do not know whether the physical characteristics of Matthew's 'Old Gregory' resembled those of the figure seen by Harriet. If we accept the theory that 'seeing a ghost' is simply an extension of one's own psychological structure, a kind of 'waking dream', then we can at once discern the point of importance in Cousin Matthew's story. It was that the figure vanished when he was forced to disturb it by extracting the Bredon Letters from the shelf in front of which it was standing. Miss Sayers knew that this would happen. The story of Cousin Matthew is precisely in accord with innumerable recorded cases, which show that when another sense is brought into play, such as that of touch in this example, the illusion is instantly destroyed and the 'ghost' disappears. In a book written by Dr E. J. Dingwall and myself, *Four Modern Ghosts* (London, 1958), which discussed certain cases coming within our own experience and was described by some critics as unduly sceptical in its approach, particularly by reviewers in spiritualistic journals, we analysed the York Museum case. The principal witness was Mr Jonas, the caretaker, who saw a figure of an elderly man in the museum library at a time when nobody should have been on the premises. Jonas described the figure as 'an odd looking chap, because he was wearing a frock-coat, drain-pipe trousers and had fluffy side-whiskers. He had very little hair and walked with a slight stoop. I decided he must be an eccentric professor.'

Jonas spoke to the figure, but received no reply, which we recall was precisely as Miss Sayers described the experience of Harriet. Jonas said in his statement:

> It was queer, but I did not think about ghosts for one minute. He looked just as real as you or me. But I did not want him roaming about so late at night, and anyway I wanted to lock up and catch my bus.

Jonas spoke to the figure again. Receiving no reply, he came to the conclusion that the curious intruder was deaf, and stretched out his hand to touch him on the shoulder. The figure instantly vanished.

The affair became complicated by much newspaper publicity (at the time I had a collection of 116 press-cuttings about the case) which in its turn precipitated a series of events only distantly connected with Jonas' experience. Suffice it to say that in our summary of the case Dr Dingwall and I remarked:

> In the first place, we have no good reason to suppose that Mr. George Jonas was romancing when he first of all told his story of the apparition. . . . His account of how the figure vanished instantaneously when he endeavoured to touch it conforms with normal expectation, in that the discovery by another sense that the figure was hallucinatory would almost always dispel a subjective apparition.

Another branch of occultism beloved by believers in the weird and wonderful is the so-called poltergeist, defined as 'a mysterous invisible agency asserted to throw things about: a noisy ghost', and frequently associated in the literature of the subject as being connected with the presence of young girls in the state of puberty. I fancy that we can judge Miss Sayers' attitude towards the reality of poltergeists from a brief passage in *Gaudy Night*, published in 1935. In the early chapters of the book, Harriet Vane pays two visits to Shrewsbury, her old college at Oxford. The first is in response to an urgent wish of an old friend, Mary Stokes, that they should attend the Shrewsbury Gaudy together. Harriet, still sensitive from the notoriety of being tried for murder, nevertheless accepts, and in general terms enjoys the occasion, which is marred only by two incidents. One is the discovery in the sleeve of her gown of a sheet of scribbling paper, with a message pasted across it made up of letters apparently cut from the headlines of newspapers. 'YOU DIRTY MURDERESS. AREN'T YOU ASHAMED TO SHOW YOUR FACE?' She was to learn at a later date that she was by no means the only recipient of such messages.

Harriet's second disagreeable experience during the Gaudy was the discovery, late one evening, of a piece of scribbling paper in the Quadrangle. On it was an ugly and sadistic drawing scrawled in pencil, depicting a naked figure of exaggeratedly female outlines, savagely assaulting a person of indeterminate sex in the cap and gown of a scholar, in a particularly humiliating fashion. It was an insane and dirty scribble. Harriet was disgusted by it and disposed of it appropriately through the suitable medium of the nearest lavatory, regretting that she had seen such a piece of filth in the precincts of Shrewsbury.

For some months she heard nothing more of her old college, until about three weeks before the end of the Easter term of the following year she received a letter from the Dean, Miss Letitia Martin, whom she had been delighted to meet again at the Gaudy. It was an invitation to attend the opening of the New Library Wing by the Chancellor of the University, Lord Oakapple. Miss Martin made it plain in her letter, however, that there was a special reason why both she and the Warden, Dr Baring, would like the benefit of a meeting with her to receive the advantage of her advice on a problem facing the College. Anonymous letters couched in obscene language were being received by both staff and students, and some deliberate damage to property had occurred, notably the making of a bonfire of a number of students' gowns in Shrewsbury Quad. As Miss Martin put it in her letter to Harriet, 'The fact is, we are being victimised by a cross between a Poltergeist and a Poison-Pen, and you can imagine how disgusting it is for everybody.'

Comment is scarcely necessary. The Dean's use of the word poltergeist in this context meant two things, or so it seems to me. Miss Martin had no belief in poltergeists in the occult sense, nor did she believe that Harriet Vane, the recipient of her letter, would take any different view. The entire text of *Gaudy Night* confirms this conclusion, which we may reasonably identify with Miss Sayers' own commonsense opinion.

Chapters XVI to XIX of Miss Sayers' *Strong Poison*, first published in 1930, tell us all we need to know, I fancy, about her attitude towards spiritualism and the supposed possibility of communication with the dead. We recall that this was the first of the four full-length Wimsey novels involving Peter's love for Harriet Vane. The story starts with her trial for the murder of her former lover, Philip Boyes. A jury disagreement results in the necessity of a second trial, which gives Wimsey time to make an investigation into the case and assemble the evidence to prove that the real murderer is Boyes' cousin, a solicitor named Norman Urquhart. I do not intend to spoil the pleasure of those persons lucky enough still to read *Strong Poison* for the first time by discussing the extremely ingenious method by which Boyes' murder is accomplished and suspicion is thrown on Harriet. My only concern is to show why four chapters are largely devoted to spiritualism, and to examine Miss Sayers' knowledge of the subject and her opinion of it.

Both Boyes and Urquhart were the great-nephews of a very old and very ill lady, Mrs Rosanna Wrayburn, whose immensely successful and somewhat scandalous stage career under the name of Cremorna Garden had enabled her to amass a considerable fortune. Urquhart was her solicitor, and in her will was appointed her executor and residuary legatee. Philip Boyes, a writer and not a man of business, was evidently her favourite relative, however, and was left £50,000 and the whole of her real estate. The motive for the murder of Boyes by Urquhart was financial, in that the latter in his capacity of executor (later with power of attorney) had recklessly squandered most of the fortune entrusted to his care by gambling on the Stock Market with heavy losses, and in particular by his deep involvement in a dubious concern called the Megatherium Trust, which had collapsed.

In 1925 Mrs Wrayburn had suffered a severe stroke, which left her completely paralysed and imbecile, which meant that her affairs were entirely in the hands of Norman Urquhart, the residuary legatee with power of attorney, but protected from exposure, disaster and criminal charges only so long as his great-aunt lived. At the date of the action of *Strong Poison* Mrs Wrayburn is over ninety, bed-ridden and helpless, in her house at Windle in Westmorland, looked after by a full-time, middle-aged nurse, Miss Caroline Booth. Mrs Wrayburn's expectation of life is obviously short, but the pre-decease of Philip Boyes saves the situation for the residuary legatee and murderer, who has stifled any suspicion of motive on his part by stating falsely (in his strong position as executor) that he has always been the sole legatee.

There are some small accessories to the main plot, including a forged draft will prepared by Urquhart to bolster his claim to be the sole beneficiary, but the point of the four chapters of the book concerned with spiritualism is that Wimsey believes (correctly) that Mrs Wrayburn's true will is somewhere in the great house at Windle, and is determined to ascertain its contents as proof of

Urquhart's possible motive for murder. For this purpose he employs his friend Miss Katherine Climpson, an elderly and astute spinster, whom we first met in *Unnatural Death*, published in 1927. She is devoted to Wimsey and his investigations, but on this occasion her task as outlined by him is a difficult one. She is to go to stay in an hotel in Windle suitable to her station in life under the pretext of looking for a small house for herself in the district. She must somehow make the acquaintance of Miss Booth, Mrs Wrayburn's resident nurse, and so insinuate herself into the house, Applefold. Once there, she must somehow find the will and ascertain its provisions.

Miss Climpson, with perseverance and considerable skill, manages to engage Miss Booth in fruitful conversation in a Windle teashop. She notices that the book Miss Booth has laid aside to talk to Miss Climpson is entitled *Can the Dead Speak?*, published by the Spiritualist Press. She also observes (is this our first clue to Miss Sayers' opinion of believers in spiritualism?) that Miss Booth possesses 'those curious large blue eyes which disconcert the beholder by their intense gaze, and are usually an index of some emotional instability'. We are told that in a single moment of illumination, Miss Climpson saw her plan of campaign complete and perfect in every detail.

Miss Climpson's knowledge of the frauds of spiritualism was considerable. As an habitué of boarding houses with other unattached spinsters and widows, she had listened for many hours to the discussion of communications from 'the other side' through the ouija board, auras, astral bodies and ectoplasmic materialisations, and against her will as a Christian but often without choice in the capacity of a paid companion, she had joined in dark séances of the table tapping and tilting variety. During a fortnight in a private hotel in Bournemouth she had met a 'quaint little man' from the 'Psychical Research Society'',[1] who had initiated her into the tricks of mediums. She knew how to turn tables and produce explosive cracking noises, and the secret of getting a 'spirit-message' on to a pair of tied and sealed slates, and many other curious secrets. Miss Climpson had wondered greatly at the folly and wickedness of mankind.

Miss Climpson was well acquainted with the literature of

[1] Presumably the Society for Psychical Research.

121

spiritualism, for she was secretly surprised that Miss Booth was unaware that the medium featured in *Can the Dead Speak?* was scarcely trustworthy. 'Surely she knows that that woman was exposed long ago?' was Miss Climpson's unspoken thought. It was helpful that Miss Booth was not mediumistic herself. 'I can't get anything when I'm alone', she said ruefully. The previous evening she had tried with the ouija board, 'but it would only write spirals'. This naturally prompted Miss Climpson to hint that she had been told by spiritualist friends that she showed unmistakable signs of mediumistic qualities. The result was an invitation to Applefold that very evening for supper and a séance from the enthusiastic Miss Booth. As Miss Climpson wrote to Lord Peter before setting out on her mission, 'I have STORMED THE CITADEL !!!'.

Having attached a small metal soap box with sticking-plaster to a strong elastic garter to place around her knee, she ensured that when squeezed sharply against her other knee the convexity of the box would emit cracks loud enough to convince the most sceptical. Miss Climpson also concealed in her sleeve, strapped to her wrist, a stout wire forming a hook strong enough to rock a light table. Thus equipped, she set out for her supper appointment, and a séance with the spirits. Her expertise reflected Miss Sayers' knowledge of the subject. While Miss Booth was up-stairs making Mrs Wrayburn comfortable for the night, Miss Climpson rapidly examined the signed photographs on the mantelpiece, and committed to memory some useful names of relatives, Miss Booth's old school, and a variety of other infor-mation for transmission from the spirit world. These were to come as knocks through the medium of a small bamboo table, the choice of which Miss Climpson heartily approved. It was the most suitable piece of furniture she could remember having seen, for the faking of 'phenomena'.

The séance was a considerable success. Communications were received from Miss Booth's girlhood sweetheart Harry, who had unfortunately 'passed over' after marrying someone else. A bad spirit calling itself 'George Washington' was disposed of quickly by Miss Climpson's 'control', who identified himself as 'Pongo'. Miss Booth's old school friend from Maidstone College, Ellen Pate (Miss Booth obligingly provided the surname) recalled dormitory feasts after lights were out, and sent love from other old friends. Before sending Miss Climpson home in the luxury of a taxi, Miss Booth insisted on a repeat performance the following evening.

At the third seance held two nights later (Miss Climpson could not bring herself to fake 'phenomena' on a Sunday) 'Pongo' introduced a new spirit who said she needed help and gave her name as 'Cremorna', amplified to Cremorna Garden, and finally as 'Rosanna Wrayburn'. At first Miss Booth suggested that Mrs Wrayburn might have died during the séance, but 'Pongo' kindly explained that this was not so. Mrs Wrayburn's spirit was 'neither in the body nor out of the body' but was 'waiting'. There was 'great trouble'. The spirit wished Miss Booth and Miss Climpson to send her will to Norman Urquhart. It was in the house, but when asked its whereabouts all the spirit could finally manage was 'In the B-B-B', followed by silence. The choice of the letter 'B' by Miss Climpson was very shrewd, because of the large field of search it offered amongst bureaux, boxes, baskets, bedrooms and so forth. Finally a black notebook was consulted, which contained a row of figures—the combination of the safe. When this was opened, the top document of the pile was the 'Will of Rosanna Wrayburn. 5 June 1920', a discovery that sealed the fate of Norman Urquhart and enabled Harriet Vane to leave the court without a stain on her character but not, for some years, to accept Peter Wimsey as her husband. The reader may think that he or she need look no further than the pages of *Strong Poison* to decide that Miss Sayers knew a great deal about spiritualism. It is of interest that among Miss Booth's books Miss Climpson noticed the title which she simply referred to as *Raymond*, which we may identify as Sir Oliver Lodge's *Raymond, or Life and Death: with Examples of Survival of Memory and Affection after Death*, published in London in 1916, with many subsequent editions. Lodge, like Sir Arthur Conan Doyle (they were knighted on the same day in 1902) was an active and devoted spiritualist. Miss Sayers was a great admirer of Doyle as the creator of Sherlock Holmes, as I have tried to show elsewhere in this book. The four chapters from *Strong Poison* that I have epitomised, however, seem to show beyond reasonable doubt what she thought about spiritualism.

INDEX OF NAMES, PLACES AND PUBLICATIONS